Shire County

NORFOLK

Margaret Knox

Shire Publications Ltd

Published in 1994 by Shire Publications Ltd, Cromwell House, Church Street, Princes Risborough, Buckinghamshire HP27 9AA, UK.
Copyright © 1994 by Margaret Knox. First published 1989. Enlarged second edition 1994.
Shire County Guide 26. ISBN 0 7478 0232 7.

Printed in Great Britain by CIT Printing Services, Press Buildings, Merlins Bridge, Haverfordwest, Dyfed SA61 1XF.

British Library Cataloguing in Publication Data:
Knox, Margaret.
Norfolk. – 2Rev.ed. – (Shire County Guide; No. 26)
I. Title II. Series
914. 26104.
ISBN 0-7478-0232-7.

Acknowledgements

Photographs are acknowledged as follows: Aerial Archaeology Publications (D. A. Edwards), page 76 (top); Great Yarmouth Publicity Department, pages 13, 25; Ruth Haynes, page 10; Margaret Knox, pages 18, 30, 33, 36 (top and bottom), 49, 79, 80, 81, 85, 86, 89 (top), 95, 99, 105, 110, 112, 114, 117, 120 (left), 131 and front cover; Cadbury Lamb, pages 7, 8, 11, 19, 21, 22, 27, 28, 37, 38, 40 (top and bottom), 41 (top and bottom), 43, 44, 45, 47, 48, 50, 52, 60, 65 (top and bottom), 68 (top and bottom), 69, 72 (top and bottom), 73, 76 (bottom), 78, 83, 87, 89 (bottom), 91 (right), 92, 93, 94, 96 (top and bottom), 100, 106, 107, 108, 111, 113, 119, 120 (right), 121, 122, 123, 124 (bottom), 130, 133, 136, 137, 139; P. R. Lange, page 127; National Trust, pages 67, 103; Norfolk Archaeological Unit (D. A. Edwards), page 75; Joanna Rees, pages 17, 82; RSPB, page 59; Anne Stevens, pages 35 (left and right), 91 (left), 124 (top); Tierney, page 39; Philip Wayre, page 127; G. N. Wright, page 97.
The maps on pages 4, 5 and 6 are by Robert Dizon. The map of Norwich on page 34 is by D. R. Darton.

Ordnance Survey grid references

Although information on how to reach most of the places described in this book by car is given in the text, National Grid References are also included in many instances, particularly for the harder-to-find places in chapters 3, 4 and 5, for the benefit of those readers who have the Ordnance Survey 1:50,000 Landranger maps of the area. The references are stated as a Landranger sheet number followed by the 100 km National Grid square and the six-figure reference.

To locate a site by means of the grid references, proceed as in the following example: Castle Acre Castle (OS 132: TF 819152). Take the OS Landranger map sheet 132 ('North West Norfolk'). The grid numbers are printed in blue around the edges of the map. (In more recently produced maps these numbers are repeated at 10 km intervals throughout the map, so that it is not necessary to open it out completely.) Read off these numbers from the left along the top edge of the map until you come to 81, denoting a vertical grid line, then estimate nine-tenths of the distance to vertical line 82 and envisage an imaginary vertical grid line 81.9 at this point. Next look at the grid numbers at one side of the map (either side will do) and read *upwards* until you find the horizontal grid line 15. Estimate two-tenths of the distance to the next horizontal line above (i.e. 16), and so envisage an imaginary horizontal line across the map at 15.2. Follow this imaginary line across the map until it crosses the imaginary vertical line 81.9. At the intersection of these two lines you will find Castle Acre Castle.

The Ordnance Survey Landranger maps which cover Norfolk are sheets 132, 133, 134, 143 and 144. Very small areas of the county are found on maps 131 and 156.

Contents

Cover: *Turf Fen Windpump at How Hill, Ludham.*

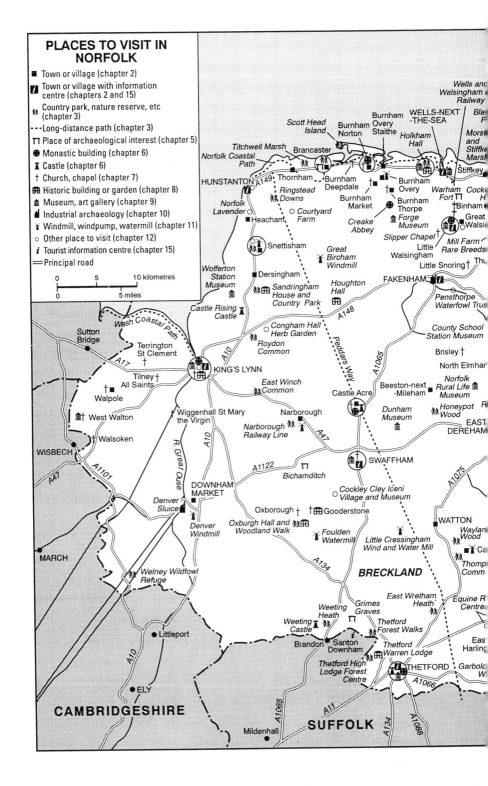

PLACES TO VISIT IN NORFOLK

- ■ Town or village (chapter 2)
- 🚹 Town or village with information centre (chapters 2 and 15)
- 🏃 Country park, nature reserve, etc (chapter 3)
- --- Long-distance path (chapter 3)
- ⊓ Place of archaeological interest (chapter 5)
- ⊕ Monastic building (chapter 6)
- 🗡 Castle (chapter 6)
- † Church, chapel (chapter 7)
- ⊞ Historic building or garden (chapter 8)
- 🏛 Museum, art gallery (chapter 9)
- 🏭 Industrial archaeology (chapter 10)
- 🗡 Windmill, windpump, watermill (chapter 11)
- ○ Other place to visit (chapter 12)
- *i* Tourist information centre (chapter 15)
- = Principal road

```
0        5        10 kilometres
|----|----|---------|
0            5 miles
|------------|
```

Wells and
Walsingham
Railway

Scott Head
Island

Titchwell Marsh
Norfolk Coastal
Path

Burnham
Norton

Burnham
Overy
Staithe

Holkham
Hall

Bla
P

WELLS-NEXT
-THE-SEA

Brancaster

Mors
and
Stiffke
Mars

HUNSTANTON A149 Thornham

Burnham
Deepdale

Ringstead
Downs

Norfolk
Lavender ○

Heacham ■

○ Courtyard
Farm

Creake
Abbey

Burnham
Market

Slipper Chapel

Stiffkey

Burnham
Overy

Warham
Fort ⊓

Cock

Binham

Burnham
Thorpe

Forge
Museum

Great
Walsi

Mill Farm
Rare Breeds

Snettisham

Great
Bircham
Windmill

Little
Walsingham ○

Little Snoring †

Thu

Wolferton
Station
Museum

■ Dersingham

Houghton
Hall

FAKENHAM

Sandringham
House and
Country Park

Castle Rising
Castle

Wash Coastal Path

Penthorpe
Waterfowl Trus

County School
Station Museum

Sutton
Bridge

Terrington
St Clement

Congham Hall
Herb Garden

Roydon
Common

KING'S LYNN

Peddars Way

Brisley †

North Elmhar

Tilney †
All Saints

Walpole

East Winch
Common

Castle Acre

Beeston-next
-Mileham

Norfolk
Rural Life 🏛
Museum

F

West Walton

Wiggenhall St Mary
the Virgin

Narborough

Dunham
Museum 🏛

Honeypot
Wood

EAST
DEREHAM

Walsoken

Narborough
Railway Line

WISBECH

A1101

A1122

Bichamditch

⊓

SWAFFHAM

Cockley Cley Iceni
○ Village and Museum

WATTON

Waylan
Wood

DOWNHAM
MARKET

Oxborough †

† ⊞ Gooderstone

Denver
Sluice

Denver
Windmill

Oxburgh Hall and
Woodland Walk

Foulden
Watermill

Ca

Little Cressingham
Wind and Water Mill

Thomp
Comm

MARCH

BRECKLAND

Welney Wildfowl
Refuge

East Wretham
Heath

Equine R
Centre

Weeting
Heath

Grimes
Graves

Littleport

Weeting
Castle

Brandon

Santon
Downham

Thetford
Forest Walks

Thetford
Warren Lodge

Eas
Harling

ELY

Thetford High
Lodge Forest
Centre

THETFORD

Garbold
W

CAMBRIDGESHIRE

Mildenhall

SUFFOLK

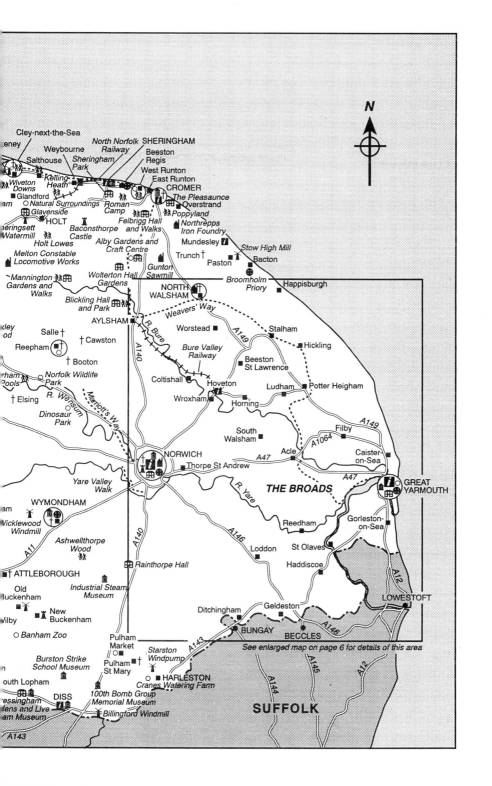

6

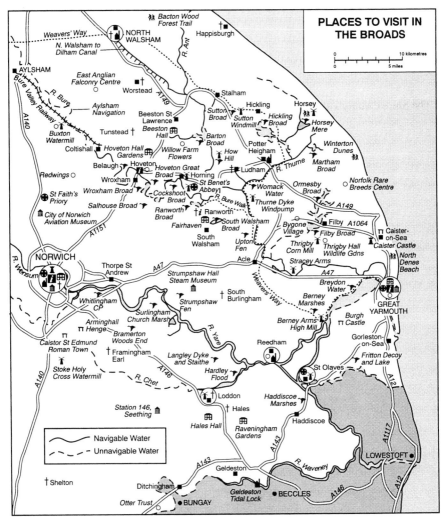

PLACES TO VISIT IN THE BROADS

0   10 kilometres
0   5 miles

- Town or village (chapter 2)
- Town or village with information centre (chapters 2 and 15)
- Country park, nature reserve etc (chapter 3)
- Country park, nature reserve etc in the Broads (chapter 4)
- ··· Long distance path (chapter 3, 4)

- ⊓ Place of archaeological interest (chapter 5)
- ● Monastic building (chapter 6)
- ⫶ Castle (chapter 6)
- † Church, chapel (chapter 7)
- ⊞ Historic building or garden (chapter 8)
- ⬛ Museum, art gallery (chapter 9)

- Industrial archaeology (chapter 10)
- ⵢ Windmill, windpump, watermill (chapter 11)
- ○ Other place to visit (chapter 12)
- *i* Tourist information centre (chapter 15)
- ══ Principal road

Navigable Water
Unnavigable Water

Preface

Welcome to the Shire County Guide to Norfolk, one of over thirty such books, written and designed to enable you to organise your time in the county well.

The Shire County Guides fill the need for a compact, accurate and thorough guide to each county so that visitors can plan a half-day excursion or a whole week's stay to best advantage. Residents, too, will find the guides a handy and reliable reference to the places of interest in their area.

Travelling British roads can be time-consuming, and the County Guides will ensure that you need not inadvertently miss any interesting feature in a locality, that you do not accidentally bypass a new museum or an outstanding church, that you can find an attractive place to picnic, and that you will appreciate the history and the buildings of the towns or villages in which you stop.

This book has been arranged in special interest chapters, such as the coast and countryside, historic buildings or archaeological sites, and all these places of interest are located on the maps on pages 4-6. Use the maps either for an overview to decide which area has most to interest you, or to help you enjoy your immediate neighbourhood. Then refer to the nearest town or village in chapter 2 to see, at a glance, what special features or attractions each community contains or is near. The subsequent chapters enable readers with a particular interest to find immediately those places of importance to them, while the cross-referencing under 'Norfolk towns and villages' assists readers with wider tastes to select how best to spend their time.

Titchwell church.

Castle Rising: the Hospital of the Most Holy and Undivided Trinity.

1
Norfolk: the place and the people

A rural way of life has survived into the twentieth century in Norfolk and, apart from the 'fine city' of Norwich and the ports of Great Yarmouth and King's Lynn, it remains a county of farms and villages, small towns and seaside resorts. The built-up area is still less than 5 per cent of the land. It is this rural aspect and the feeling it gives of 'being in the country' that makes Norfolk an attractive place to live in and to visit. The industrial revolution all but passed Norfolk by and this, with its relative isolation from the rest of Britain, has helped to preserve its distinctiveness, its strong regional accent and a reputation for 'doing different'.

Norfolk sticks out into the North Sea and is open to its harsh winds and wild winter rages; it has also been open to centuries of invasions and influence from the countries of northern Europe. Flying in to Norwich Airport from Amsterdam, it seems only a stone's throw from its continental neighbours. The flight path crosses the coast at Great Yarmouth above the Denes and continues over Broadland's maze of waterways, marshes and fields, a flat landscape dotted with churches, windmills and windpumps. It is not unlike the landscape left behind in the Low Countries.

Rocks and soils

Norfolk is not quite as flat as it at first appears. Underlying the land mass is a substratum of chalk overlaid by crags, and above that are glacial deposits of sand and gravel. There are low hills and heaths stretching from Thetford to Holme on the coast and the Holt Ridge from Sheringham to Cromer rises to Norfolk's highest point (340 feet, 102 metres) at West Runton. The chalk comes to the surface only in the western half of the county, for example at a disused quarry at Ringstead Downs, although at Whitwell ('white well') near Reepham it shows itself in spring water and it can be seen on the beach at West Runton. At Great Yarmouth the chalk is 500 feet (150 metres) below the surface.

Older strata come to the surface at Hunstanton. Here, at low tide, dark Kimmeridge clay can be seen on the shore. It is overlaid with carrstone, the 'gingerbread' rock, then by Hunstanton's 'red rock', pink in colour, and then by the much younger chalk, forming the famous striped cliffs.

Further west in Marshland the countryside is flat and featureless; Broadland too is flat but not without contours, and south of Norwich the heavy clays, overlaid on crags, rarely rise above 200 feet (60 metres). Stone for building is in short supply, apart from rock formerly quarried around Hunstanton, but flints are plentiful and have given Norfolk its distinctive architecture. Brick earths are found in pockets everywhere except in Marshland, and Norfolk brickwork is among the finest in England.

The climate

Norfolk is the sunniest and driest part of England and its huge skies above a low horizon have inspired generations of artists. Winters are often bleak, with searing winds from across the North Sea causing trees in coastal areas to be misshapen, and snow is not unusual.

Cornlands and sheep pastures

The gentle contours, easily worked soils and the climate have made Norfolk eminently suitable for farming. Corn has always been important but in the middle ages pastures on enclosed land on the lighter soils supported vast flocks of sheep, which were the basis of the important weaving industry. Wetlands were drained to provide more pastures and much later, in the eighteenth century, the need to increase production on the light soils of west Norfolk, where two rabbits were said to fight for one blade of grass, led to the agricultural improvements pioneered by Coke of Holkham. Perhaps Norfolk's greatest contribution to the prosperity of Britain has been in the field of agriculture.

In the twentieth century crop production has reached new levels of efficiency as a result of mechanisation and the use of agrochemicals, but at a cost to the environment. Increase in field size has caused the loss of hedges and woodland, mixed farming has declined in wetlands and pastures have come under the plough, and watercourses have been polluted. But the mood is changing and farmers and the general public are becoming increasingly concerned about the natural environment.

Breckland

Not all of Norfolk has disappeared under the plough. The county still has some of the best nature reserves in Britain – on the coast, in Broadland and in Breckland. Breckland is an area of about 25 million acres (10 million ha)

of sandy gravelly soils stretching across south-west Norfolk into Suffolk. It is an area of low rainfall and extremes of temperature and has many of the characteristics of continental heaths and steppes. Marshes or small lakes are found throughout Breckland, fed from the chalk below.

Between the world wars large areas of the heath were planted with conifers by the Forestry Commission, totally changing parts of the landscape. The timber is now being harvested and belts of deciduous woodland are being introduced when the land is replanted. Breckland also has a large Ministry of Defence battle area and this ironically is now a valuable nature reserve, having been protected from the ravages of intensive farming.

The coast

The coast of Norfolk sweeps round in a smooth curve without deep estuaries, from the Wash to Great Yarmouth, for almost 100 miles (160 km). The Wash is less extensive now than when King John lost his jewels there in the thirteenth century, reclamation having been continuous since Roman times. There are saltmarshes, mudflats and sand-dunes from the Wash to the low cliffs at

The famous striped cliffs at Hunstanton.

The lifeboat station on the beach at Wells-next-the-Sea.

Hunstanton and again from Holme to Weybourne, and tiny rivers weave their way through muddy estuaries to the sea. This is an area much loved by naturalists and yachtsmen. From Weybourne to Mundesley there are cliffs of unstable glacial material, rich in fossils. Here cliff falls are not unusual in winter. South from Happisburgh the cliffs disappear, and there are sand and shingle beaches, although sand cliffs are forming at Scratby. The relentless power of the sea is a fact of life in Norfolk, as the 1953 floods demonstrated. Erosion of the coastline is taking place at a rate of 1 to 5 yards (1 to 4.5 metres) a year, aided by the fact that the land is tipping towards the east and sea level is rising. Further losses of land seem inevitable in the future.

Fishing

There have been fishing communities along the coast since earliest times. Winterton and Great Yarmouth began as winter camps for fishermen catching shoal fish as they moved south. From Roman times there were salt pans on the coast, the salt being used to preserve the fish. Shoal fishing for herring and mackerel reached its zenith in the nineteenth century and by the beginning of the twentieth century there was a huge herring industry using steam drifters and based on east coast ports, Great Yarmouth being one of the most important, but overfishing led to the collapse of the industry after the Second World War.

Today shellfish rather than wet fish are important — shrimps and cockles in the Wash, whelks and mussels in north Norfolk and lobsters and crabs at Cromer and Sheringham. Only on the coast from Winterton to Yarmouth is inshore line fishing for cod, whiting, plaice and dabs still important.

Smoked fish has long been a speciality: kippers and bloaters were almost synonymous with Yarmouth and small smoke-houses still operate, for example at Cley.

Slow-flowing rivers

The rivers of Norfolk are slow-flowing and shallow, meandering through meadows often only a few feet above sea level. They rise in chalk and everywhere, except in the peaty fens, the water is hard. The Yare and Wensum, with their tributaries the Ant, Bure, Chet and Thurne, flow through Broadland to reach the sea at Yarmouth. The Waveney forms the county's southern boundary and also flows into the sea at Yarmouth. The Little Ouse rises just a short distance from the source of the Waveney near the Suffolk border but flows west to join the Great Ouse and enter the sea at King's Lynn. Norfolk's rivers are quiet and compliant most of the time, amenable to being diverted by means of canals, dykes and cuts, but flooding is an ever present danger, and without drains and dykes, sluices and pumps there would be more floods and much less agricultural land in Norfolk.

The Broads

The waterways of Broadland are unique in Europe – 200 miles (320 km) of navigable water with no locks. There are more than thirty broads, irregularly shaped lakes that were formed as a result of peat diggings between the twelfth and fourteenth centuries, a fact not fully understood until research was published in 1960. The peat was used as domestic fuel and for making salt from sea water. The diggings became flooded in the later middle ages when sea level rose. Long before peat digging began, villages had been established in the area on outcrops of the crags and the older parts of villages such as Ranworth are situated on slight hills. Wells dug into the crag supplied the villages with pure water. After the Broads were formed these settlements grew alongside the new waterways.

For centuries the clear and beautiful waters of the Broads were used simply for transport and fishing, and reeds and sedge were harvested for use as thatch. Painters such as John Crome and John Sell Cotman and the photographer P. H. Emerson delighted in recording their wild beauty. It was not until the 1870s and the coming of the railways that the Broads were discovered by holidaymakers. Today it is their value for recreation and as a habitat for wildlife, including such rare species as the bittern and the swallowtail butterfly, that is of overriding importance. In 1988 the Broads Act was passed giving the area special status equivalent to that of a national park and the Broads Authority was given powers to protect the fragile environment, improve recreational facilities and generally assume a protective role.

Norfolk through the ages

The Norfolk landscape is almost entirely man-made, even such apparently natural areas like the Broads. The people who created what we see today began arriving a million years ago. The first stone age people settled in Breckland on the dry heathland and they excavated and worked the flint mines which supplied tools to neolithic tribes in other parts of England. One of their mines, at Grimes Graves near Weeting, can still be seen (see page 75). Some groups moved into river valleys and to the coast of Norfolk and by the bronze age settlements were widely scattered, as burial sites confirm.

Iron age skills were brought to Norfolk by the Iceni and under King Prasutagus and his widow Queen Boudicca (Boadicea) a well-organised kingdom was established in East Anglia. One of the first recorded historic events in Norfolk is the revolt of the Iceni against the invading Romans in AD 60. The Warham iron age fort and the Roman town at Caistor St Edmund date from this time. Most of the Roman remains in Norfolk have been obliterated by cultivation but there are the ruins of a castle at Burgh near Yarmouth and of a coastal fort at Brancaster. By AD 425 the Romans had departed and Anglo-Saxon raids intensified. In the turbulent centuries that followed many skills known to the Romanised population were lost but by the seventh century society had stabilised and become Christian. Thetford was the main centre and many villages already had the names and shape that we know today.

Raids by the Danes or Vikings began in AD 841 and Danish settlement followed, especially in Broadland in the area known as the Fleggs (a Scandinavian word for reeds), where place-names ending in -by ('settlement') are common. It was the waves of Nordic invaders who gave the Norfolk people their physical characteristics. Even today there is a preponderance of blue eyes, fair and freckled skins and people with a tall solid build.

By the end of the Saxon period Norwich had supplanted Thetford as the main centre and Great Yarmouth already had a merchant community. Domesday Book shows that Norfolk was the most densely populated area of England in the eleventh century and it was to grow in wealth and importance throughout the medieval period.

Medieval Norfolk

After the Norman Conquest in the eleventh century, farming prospered, the move away from the dry heathlands accelerated and towns expanded. Architecture progressed under the managerial and technological skills brought by the Normans: Norwich Castle and Cath-

The quayside at Great Yarmouth.

edral were built, and many parish churches, of which some survive, for example at Hales and South Lopham. As the middle ages progressed, the Norman overlords and the Saxon population merged to some extent but the landowners, merchants and clergy were predominantly Norman. Norfolk had become wealthy, at first through the leather industry and then from weaving, using local wool and the skill of Flemish immigrant workers who began to arrive in Norman times and came in large numbers in the Tudor period. The trade in woollen cloth made Norwich the sixth richest city in England in the fourteenth century and the prosperity of Great Yarmouth and King's Lynn expanded. The medieval guildhalls, merchants' houses, manor houses, monasteries and magnificent 'wool' churches that we still see today testify to the prosperity of the late middle ages. The cloth, much of it worsted (named after the village of Worstead), was woven in tiny workshops and it was the wool dealers, the master weavers and the cloth merchants, rather than the ordinary weavers, who grew rich.

Social and religious upheavals

Throughout the middle ages and the Tudor period the rich were getting richer, the poor poorer. In 1549 the Kett brothers from Wymondham led a rebellion in protest at the injustices suffered by the lower classes, a rebellion sparked off by the enclosure of common land. The revolt was put down and the inequalities of wealth increased. By the early seventeenth century it is said that four-fifths of the population of Norwich were poor or destitute. The social unrest and political and religious turmoil culminated in the Civil War in 1642, which split the county into rival camps; King's Lynn was for the King, Norwich and Great Yarmouth for Parliament; the Pastons, le Stranges, Bedingfields and Heydons were among those for the King, the Hobarts of Blickling, the Astleys of Melton Constable and the Cokes of Holkham for Parliament. The beautiful medieval churches which had suffered after the Reformation were again desecrated by the Puritans. At the end of the Civil War Parliament and the Puritan faction were in the ascendancy but the established religion no longer had the hold on the people that it had had in the middle ages and many parish churches fell into ruins, to be restored, often with less than happy results, by the Victorians.

Stately homes

In spite of the turmoil, those county families that had been Parliamentarians and escaped sequestration of their property prospered and during the following two centuries built themselves mansions and laid out parks, the most notable being Blickling, Gunton, Holkham, Houghton, Melton Constable and Raynham.

It was, however, an era of decline in Norfolk as the industrial revolution carried industry northwards to sources of power that Norfolk lacked. A new impetus came in the eighteenth century from the agricultural revolution, led by Coke, which increased food production and helped feed the growing urban population of England. The eighteenth and nineteenth centuries were a time of stability and stagnation in Norfolk although nonconformity in religion grew, radical politics were in the air and there was a scattered flowering of intellectual talent. William Cowper, the poet, came from East Dereham; Robert Walpole was from Houghton and Elizabeth Fry was from a Norwich Quaker family.

The railway era

The first railway opened in Norfolk in 1844 and soon the county was criss-crossed by rival lines. The railways caused more social upheaval than industrial development and brought the first visitors to the new seaside resorts. People continued to move away from the villages into the larger towns, and Norwich, King's Lynn and Yarmouth spread far beyond their medieval walls.

Norfolk in the twentieth century

In the twentieth century, particularly since the two world wars, Norfolk has been subjected to many new influences. A group of Scottish farmers arrived in the 1930s, backed by the Bank of Scotland, to revitalise some of Norfolk's failing farms; military airfields brought an influx of servicemen, many of them American, during and after the Second World War, and the London overspill after the war swelled the populations of King's Lynn and Thetford. New people and new ideas have also come with the setting up of the University of East Anglia at Norwich in 1964 and the development of the North Sea oil and gas industry, with shore facilities at Great Yarmouth and Bacton. Britain's entry into the European Community and the growth of tourism have helped to make East Anglia the fastest-growing region in Britain today. It is to be hoped that development will be controlled and Norfolk will be able to retain its rural traditions and the feeling it gives of 'being in the country'.

2
Norfolk towns and villages

Acle
Early closing Wednesday; market day Thursday.
This small town halfway between Norwich and Great Yarmouth on the river Bure is a centre for farmers, fruit growers (the area is rich in 'pick-your-own' farms) and the Broadland tourist industry. The river is tidal and there are boatyards for servicing and hiring boats. A new bridge carries the A1064 over the river – the only crossing between Wroxham and Yarmouth. There are good shops and the weekly market is a good hunting ground for bric-à-brac and antiques as well as local farm produce.
In the locality: Breydon Water Local Nature Reserve, page 64; Cockshoot Broad, page 64; How Hill, pages 67 and 121; South Walsham Broad, page 70; Ranworth Broad and Conservation Centre, page 70; Strumpshaw Fen Nature Reserve, page 70; Surlingham Church Marsh, page 70; Upton Fen, page 71; St Benet's Abbey, page 81; churches at Ranworth, page 91; and South Burlingham, page 94; Fairhaven Garden Trust, page 99; Strumpshaw Hall Steam Museum, page 111; Berney Arms High Mill, page 118; St Benet's Abbey Mill, page 122; Stracey Arms Windpump, page 123.

Alby
Alby Gardens, page 98; Alby Craft Centre, page 125.

Arminghall
Arminghall Henge Monument, page 74.

Ashwellthorpe
Ashwellthorpe Wood, page 56.

Attleborough
Early closing Wednesday; market day Thursday.
Attleborough is famous for its cider works and turkeys. It once had an annual turkey fair, following which the flocks of turkeys were walked to London along the Great Post Road, now the A11, which bypasses the town. The war memorial in the centre of Attleborough commemorates those who died in the battle of Inkerman (1856) in the Crimean War. There is also a fine church.
Church of the Assumption, page 84.
In the locality: Ashwellthorpe Wood, page 56; East Wretham Heath, page 57; Thompson Common, page 62; Wayland Wood, page 62; Wymondham Abbey, page 83; church at Wilby, page 97; Wymondham Heritage Museum, page 114; Banham Zoo, page 125. See also the Buckenhams, page 18; Watton, page 53; Wymondham, page 55.

Aylsham
Early closing Wednesday; market days (including auction sales) Tuesday and Friday.
The open market place is surrounded by handsome eighteenth-century buildings including the Queen Anne Black Boy inn. One house has a plaque commemorating Christopher Layer, a Jacobite martyr. Aylsham was a weaving town in the late middle ages and enjoyed prosperity again after the opening of the navigation (see page 115), which made the Bure navigable from Coltishall to Aylsham. It is still a busy market town and also has nationally important antique auctions. The church of St Michael has flint flushwork decoration and in the churchyard there is a memorial to Humphry Repton (see page 137).
In the locality: Blickling Park Walks, page 56; Mannington Walks, page 58; Baconsthorpe Castle, page 77; churches at Booton, page 84; Cawston, page 85; North Walsham, page 88; Reepham, page 91; Salle, page 91; Tunstead, page 95; and Worstead, page 97; Alby Gardens, page 98; Blickling

Hall, page 98; Mannington Gardens, page 101; Wolterton Hall Gardens, page 103; Bure Valley Railway, page 115; Gunton Sawmill, page 116; Melton Constable Locomotive Works, page 116; Alby Craft Centre, page 125.

Baconsthorpe
Castle, page 77.

Bacton
The huge North Sea gas installation, partly hidden behind grass embankments, has brought employment to this quiet seaside town, but it is none the less an intrusion into an area of great natural beauty. Bacton has long sandy beaches which are completely covered at high tide but at low tide there are pools for paddling and good sand. Fishermen operate from offshore boats at Bacton Gap. In the town there are plenty of cafés and amusements for holidaymakers. The ruins of Broomholm Priory can be seen on the outskirts and many cottages incorporate stones from the ruins in their walls.

Bacton Wood Forest Trail, page 56; **Broomholm Priory**, page 77.

In the locality: Felbrigg Lakeside and Woodland Walks, page 57; churches at Happisburgh, page 87; North Walsham, page 88; and Trunch, page 94; Alby Gardens, page 98; Beeston Hall and Gardens, page 98; Felbrigg Hall, page 100; Wolterton Hall Gardens, page 103; Stow High Windmill, page 123; Alby Craft Centre, page 125. See also Cromer, page 20; Mundesley, page 32; North Walsham, page 32.

Banham
Banham Zoo and Monkey Sanctuary, page 125.

Barton
Barton Broad, page 64.

Beeston
There are three widely separated Beestons in Norfolk, all of them villages. **Beeston-next-Mileham** between Swaffham and East Dereham has a fine church and was a dormitory town for American airmen serving on Wend-

ling Airfield in the Second World War. **Beeston Regis** stands on the cliff in north Norfolk with the heath to landward. There are the remains of an Augustinian priory in the village. **Beeston St Lawrence** is a pretty village in Broadland. The hall and gardens are open to the public.

Beeston Regis Heath, page 60; **Beeston St Lawrence Hall and Gardens**, page 98.

Belaugh
Broadland village, page 64.

Billingford
Near Scole. Billingford Windmill, page 118.

Binham
Pretty flint cottages and elegant houses are set around a green in this attractive west Norfolk village just 3 miles (5 km) from the sea. Many of them contain stones plundered from the priory. There is also the stump of an old cross on the green, another reminder of the Christian past of this corner of Norfolk.

Binham Priory, page 77.

In the locality: Blakeney Point, page 56; Cley Marshes, page 56; Holt Lowes Country Park, page 58; Morston and Stiffkey Marshes, page 58; Salthouse Marsh Nature Reserve, page 60; Wiveton Downs Picnic Area, page 63; Warham Iron Age Fort, page 75; Baconsthorpe Castle, page 77; Walsingham Abbey, page 83; churches at Blakeney, page 84; the Burnhams, page 84; Cley, page 85; and Little Snoring, page 88; Holkham Hall and Gardens, page 100; Cockthorpe Hall Toy Museum, page 104; Thursford Museum, page 113; Wells and Walsingham Light Railway, page 117; Letheringsett Watermill, page 121; Langham Glass, page 127. See also Blakeney, below; Holt, page 27; the Walsinghams, page 52; Wells-next-the-Sea, page 53.

Blakeney
Early closing Wednesday.
In summer small boats, mostly yachts and pleasure craft, crowd this small port at the mouth of the river Glaven. At low tide there is a wide expanse of mudflats with the river trickling through but at high tide boats can

Blakeney: the quay.

sail into the harbour. The saltmarshes between the town and the sea attract walkers and naturalists, and Blakeney Point is only a short boat ride away. The town itself has narrow lanes of flint cottages tumbling down to the harbour wall, good hotels and shops, a fine church and a medieval guildhall. Blakeney is a most attractive town, perhaps saved from overdevelopment because a proposed railway link failed to materialise.

Blakeney Point, page 56; **church of St Nicholas**, page 84; **Guildhall**, page 98

In the locality: Cley Marshes, page 56; Morston and Stiffkey Marshes, page 58; Holt Lowes Country Park, page 58; Salthouse Marsh Nature Reserve, page 60; Wiveton Downs Picnic Area, page 63; Warham Iron Age Fort, page 75; Binham Priory, page 77; Walsingham Abbey, page 83; churches at the Burnhams, page 84; and Cley, page 85; Holkham Hall and Gardens, page 100; Cockthorpe Hall Toy Museum, page 104; Wells and Walsingham Light Railway, page 117; Letheringsett Watermill, page 121; Langham Glass, page 127. See also Holt, page 27; Wells-next-the-Sea, page 53; and the Walsinghams, page 52.

Brancaster

The name hints at a Roman connection and Brancaster was indeed the site of an important coastal fortress in Roman times. Now the creeks are popular with sailing enthusiasts and many of the fishermen's cottages are holiday homes. The seventeenth-century Dial House at Brancaster Staithe (now used by the National Trust's coastal warden) and the eighteenth-century Staithe House are reminders that this was once a prosperous small port. Now the sea has retreated, leaving a quiet sandy beach, saltmarshes and dunes.

Brancaster Manor Recreation Area, page 56; **Roman Fort**, page 74.

In the locality: Holkham National Nature Reserve, page 57; Scolt Head Island National Nature Reserve, page 61; Titchwell Marsh Nature Reserve, page 62; Warham Iron Age Fort, page 75; Binham Priory, page 77; Creake Abbey, page 79; Walsingham Abbey, page 83; churches at the Burnhams, page 84; and Cley, page 85; Walsingham Slipper Chapel, page 95; Holkham Hall, page 100; Wells and Walsingham Light Railway, page 117; Great Bircham Windmill, page 120; Snettisham Watermill, page 122; Norfolk Lav-

The market house, New Buckenham.

ender, *page 127; Park Farm, Snettisham,
page 128. See also Hunstanton, page 29;
Wells-next-the-Sea, page 53.*

The Buckenhams

The original Buckenham in south Norfolk
became Old Buckenham in 1136 when the
Norman castle was removed to a new site and
New Buckenham was created as a planned
village built on a grid of intersecting streets.
It is a unique survival in England of a planned
medieval village. The castle was demolished
in 1640 but the village became a market town
clustered around one of the largest village
greens in Norfolk. Now it is a quiet village
once again but some grand houses survive, as
does the late sixteenth-century market house,
complete with whipping post. The church of
St Martin has a fifteenth-century tower with
flushwork and a wealth of interesting detail
inside. A village trail leaflet is available at
the village shop. Old Buckenham also has a
large green with the thatched church of All
Saints nearby.

New Buckenham Castle, page 79; **Old**

Buckenham Cornmill, page 122.

*In the locality: churches at Attleborough,
page 84; East Harling, page 86; Pulham St
Mary, page 90; South Lopham, page 94; and
Wilby, page 97; Bressingham Gardens and
Live Steam Museum, pages 99 and 104;
Burston Strike School Museum, page 104;
100th Bomb Group Memorial Museum, page
112; Billingford Windmill, page 118; Starston
Windpump, page 122; Banham Zoo, page 125;
Pulham Market Vineyard, page 129.*

The Burnhams

This cluster of seven Burnham villages is an
extreme example of the subdivision of parishes that took place in wealthy areas in the
early middle ages. Burnham Market is the
most prosperous of the seven and its wide
village street and greens are lined with elegant houses, flint cottages and interesting
little shops. There is an important craft market here in August. Burnham Thorpe, further
inland, was Nelson's birthplace (see page
132). Burnham Overy has attractive old
maltings, two windmills, a watermill and a

mill house. The river Burn finally makes its way to the sea at Burnham Overy Staithe after wandering through creeks and saltmarshes. This village is much loved by naturalists and sailing enthusiasts. At Burnham Norton there is a ruined friary and several of the villages have interesting churches.

Burnham Norton Friary, page 78; **the churches**, page 84; **Burnham Overy Windmill**, page 118.

In the locality: Holkham National Nature Reserve, page 57; Morston and Stiffkey Marshes, page 58; Scolt Head Island National Nature Reserve, page 61; Binham Priory, page 77; churches at Blakeney, page 84; Cley, page 85; and Little Snoring, page 88; Walsingham Slipper Chapel, page 95; Holkham Hall, page 100; Houghton Hall, page 101; Bygones at Holkham, page 107; Forge Museum, page 109; Shirehall Museum, page 113; Wells and Walsingham Light Railway, page 117; Langham Glass, page 127; Textile Centre, Great Walsingham, page 129.

Caister-on-Sea

This village just 2 miles (3 km) north of Great Yarmouth existed long before its larger neighbour became a town. It owes its name to the fortified settlement built by the Romans. Later the Normans built a castle here and the family of Falstaffe, made famous by Shakespeare, lived there during the middle ages and in Tudor times. The castle is now a car museum. Today Caister-on-Sea is a tourist centre with holiday camps and caravan sites.

Roman Town, page 74; **Caister Castle and Car Collection**, page 78.

Caistor St Edmund

Roman Town, page 74.

Castle Acre

Castle Acre has four important historical monuments, including a Norman castle and the remains owed of a Cluniac monastery. The village owed its importance to its proximity to the medieval shrine at Walsingham but its earlier history is enshrined in the tiny Saxon church of All Saints, which has survived almost untouched. After the Reformation, Castle Acre declined but even in late Victorian times it was still a busy community with rural craft workshops, a tannery and a brickyard. Today the population is 700.

Bailey Gate, page 78; **Castle**, page 78; **Priory**, page 78; **church**, page 85.

Castle Acre: the Bailey Gate.

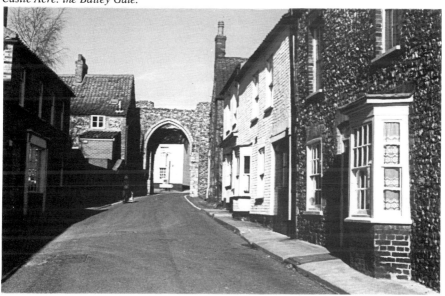

Castle Rising

Castle, page 78.

Caston

Caston, near Watton in south-west Norfolk, is only a small village but it is popular with visitors because of its fine windmill. The village has also won the best-kept village award and its thatched church, standing by the village green, is most attractive.
Caston Windmill, page 119.

Cawston

Church, page 85.

Cley-next-the-Sea

The coast road pushes its way through the narrow streets of the village (the name Cley rhymes with 'sky'), between flint cottages and houses dating from the eighteenth and nineteenth centuries. This was once an important wool port but after the sixteenth century the port declined. The quay near the windmill and the old eighteenth-century custom house are reminders of past glory. Local fishermen catch shellfish and inshore wet fish and there is a smoke-house. Cley is a popular holiday centre; visitors enjoy the traditional atmosphere of pubs like the Fishmongers' Arms and the Harnser (a Norfolk word for heron), the old-fashioned shops, lokes (lanes), courtyards and flint cottages. Between the village and the sea there are saltmarshes and sand-dunes and a nature reserve; 'twitchers' come in their hundreds all the year round to see the great variety of bird life. There is a beautiful fourteenth-century church.
Cley Marshes, page 56; **church**, page 85; **Cley Windmill**, page 119.
In the locality: Blakeney Point, page 56; Holt Lowes Country Park, page 58; Kelling Heath Nature Trail, page 58; Morston and Stiffkey Marshes, page 58; Salthouse Marsh Nature Reserve, page 60; Wiveton Downs Picnic Area, page 63; Warham Iron Age Fort, page 75; Baconsthorpe Castle, page 77; Binham Priory, page 77; Walsingham Abbey, page 83; churches at Blakeney, page 84; and Little Snoring, page 88; Walsingham Slipper Chapel, page 95; Felbrigg Hall, page 100; Holkham Hall and Gardens, page 100; Cock-

thorpe Hall Toy Museum, page 104; Bygones at Holkham, page 107; Shirehall Museum, page 113; North Norfolk Railway, page 116; Wells and Walsingham Light Railway, page 117; Letheringsett Watermill, page 121. See also Blakeney, page 16; Cromer, below; Holt, page 27; Sheringham, page 47.

Cockley Cley

Iceni Village and Museums, page 125.

Cockthorpe

Cockthorpe Hall Toy Museum, page 104.

Coltishall

Coltishall is an attractive village on the river Bure on the edge of Broadland and is popular with visitors. From the sixteenth century to the eighteenth the town became a thriving wherry port and in the eighteenth century the river was made navigable to Aylsham, bringing more trade. After the railway was opened the river trade collapsed, but finally the railway also closed. Today the village is busy once again, especially in summer. There are boating facilities, pretty walks by the river, an interesting thatched church and good antique and craft shops.
In the locality: the Broads, chapter 4, page 64; churches at North Walsham, page 88; Tunstead, page 95; and Worstead, page 97; Blickling Hall, page 98; Hoveton Hall Gardens, page 101; North Walsham to Dilham Canal, page 116; Redwings Horse Sanctuary, page 129. See also Aylsham, page 15; North Walsham, page 32; Norwich, page 32; Wroxham, page 54.

Cromer

Early closing Wednesday.
Until Victorian times Cromer was just a fishing village perched on high cliffs and backed by woods and low hills. The railway brought visitors and it became a high-class seaside resort. The Victorian and Edwardian hotels and boarding houses and the grand vacation houses built by the wealthy still dominate the town. Today Cromer is a popular resort with amusement arcades, an August carnival, a summer theatre on the pier, and gardens and amusements on the promenade. The church

Dersingham: the carrstone and brick barn.

and museums are worth visiting and the beach is full of interest, with ridges of sand and shingle, breakwaters and rock pools at low tide. Fishermen catch inshore fish, lobsters and crabs (a local speciality) and from below the Gangway and to the east there are lovely walks on the clifftop to the lighthouse and beyond.

Church of St Peter and St Paul, page 86; **Cromer Museum**, page 104; **Old Boathouse Lifeboat Museum**, page 104.

In the locality: Poppyland, page 59; churches at Cley, page 85; and Trunch, page 94; Felbrigg Hall, page 100; The Pleasaunce, page 102; North Norfolk Railway, page 116; Northrepps Iron Foundry and Sawpit, page 116; Stow High Windmill, page 123. See also Overstrand, page 42; Sheringham, page 47.

Denver

Denver Sluice, page 115; Denver Windmill, page 119.

Dereham

See East Dereham, page 23.

Dersingham

This large village in west Norfolk, which has more than 3000 inhabitants, is close to the royal estate at Sandringham and has views over sandy heaths and the Wash. Now protected from the busy A149 by a bypass, it is returning to its quiet old ways. The church of St Nicholas has a painted screen and a magnificent carved parish chest dating to the fourteenth century; nearby is a barn built of the local carrstone and red brick.

In the locality: Ringstead Downs, page 60; Roydon Common, page 60; Snettisham Nature Reserve, page 61; Scolt Head Island National Nature Reserve, page 61; Titchwell Marsh Nature Reserve, page 62; Castle Rising Castle, page 78; Houghton Hall, page 101; Sandringham House, Museum and Country Park, page 102; Great Bircham Windmill, page 120; Norfolk Lavender, page 127. See also Hunstanton, page 29; and King's Lynn, page 29.

Dickleburgh

100th Bomb Group Memorial Museum, page 112.

Diss

Early closing Tuesday.

Sir John Betjeman preferred Diss to any other

Diss Museum.

English town. One of its attractions is the maze of streets clustered round the church, where there are sixteenth-century timber-framed houses with gables and jutting upper storeys as well as houses of the eighteenth and nineteenth centuries. One reason for the survival of the quaint old-style houses is that Diss, unlike most English towns, escaped a major fire in Tudor times. The mere alongside one of the streets is another attraction. The town is growing fast as it has the advantage of good rail and road links out of the region. John Skelton, the poet, was rector here in the sixteenth century (see page 135) and Mary Wilson, wife of Harold Wilson, the former Prime Minister, lived here as a child. There is a good antique centre and a museum.

Diss Museum, page 105.

In the locality: New Buckenham Castle, page 79; churches at Attleborough, page 84; East Harling, page 86; Pulham St Mary, page 90; South Lopham, page 94; and Wilby, page 97; Bressingham Gardens and Live Steam Museum, pages 99 and 104; Industrial Steam Museum, page 105; 100th Bomb Group Memorial Museum, page 112; Billingford Windmill, page 118; Garboldisham Windmill, page 120; Starston Windpump, page 122; Banham Zoo, page 125; Pulham Market Vineyard, page 129. See also Attleborough, page 15; Harleston, page 26; and Thetford, page 51.

Ditchingham

There has been a settlement at Ditchingham on the banks of the Waveney since neolithic times, as evidenced by a burial mound found on a gravel terrace by the river. Today it is a large and growing village, and almost a suburb of the small town of Bungay on the Suffolk bank of the river. The eighteenth-century hall stands in a park with a lake, the result of landscaping by 'Capability' Brown, and Ditchingham House – once the home of Rider Haggard (see page 136) – is now the Anglican convent of All Hallows. There are walks by the river at the foot of the Bath Hills (36 feet or 11 metres!) – the highest point in Broadland.

In the locality: churches at Hales, page 87; Pulham St Mary, page 90; and Shelton, page 94; Geldeston Tidal Lock, page 115; Billingford Windmill, page 118; Starston Windpump, page 122; Otter Trust, page 128; Pulham Market Vineyard, page 129. See also Geldeston.

Downham Market
Early closing Wednesday; market days Fridays and Saturdays.

This is the major town and shopping centre for the area on the eastern edge of the fen in west Norfolk. It stands on slightly higher ground than the rich agricultural area that it serves. Much of the town is built of carrstone from quarries to the east of the town and there are some notable old buildings, some showing Dutch influence. The market place is dominated by the Gothic clock (1878). Downham was once a sizable inland port but the railway and a new canal cut off the town from the river. Now there are pleasant walks on the riverbank but little river traffic. The carrstone church stands on a hillock surrounded by a pretty churchyard.

In the locality: Welney Wildfowl Refuge, page 63; Bichamditch, page 74; church at Wiggenhall St Mary the Virgin, page 95; Oxburgh Hall and Gardens, page 102; Denver Sluice, page 115; Denver Windmill, page 119.

East Dereham

Early closing Wednesday; market days Tuesdays and Fridays.

East Dereham is right in the middle of Norfolk and a busy market town. Its name originates from the herds of deer once common here. St Withburga's Lane leads to the church and also to the Bishop Bonner Museum. There are interesting eighteenth-century buildings around the market, suggesting more prosperous times, and a disused railway track crosses the town. There is a thriving industrial park on the outskirts. Dereham has literary connections: William Cowper, the poet, was born here and George Borrow (the author of *Lavengro*) was born at a farmhouse at Dumpling Green (see page 135).

Church of St Nicholas, page 86; **Bishop Bonner Cottages Museum,** page 105; **Dereham Windmill,** page 119.

In the locality: Hoe Rough, page 57; Honeypot Wood Nature Reserve, page 58; Sparham Pools, page 61; Castle Acre Bailey Gate, Castle and Priory, page 78; North Elmham Saxon Cathedral and Bishop's Castle, page 80; churches at Brisley, page 84; Elsing, page 87; and North Elmham, page 88; Norfolk Rural Life Museum, page 107; Dunham Museum, page 108; County School Station Museum, page 109; Elmham Park Vineyards and Winery, page 126; Norfolk Wildlife Park, page 128.

East Harling

This large village on the Norfolk-Suffolk border has a population of over 2000 and is an important rural centre with shops, a school and medical services. The centre of the village has fine Georgian buildings and has been designated a conservation area. Sir John Betjeman described the church as 'a riot of splendour' and it is one of the finest in Norfolk.

Church of St Peter and St Paul, page 86.

East Runton

See the Runtons, page 43.

East Wretham

East Wretham Heath, page 57.

Fakenham

Early closing Wednesday; market days Thursday and Saturday.

Around the large market place of this busy town on the river Wensum north-west of Norwich there are handsome eighteenth- and nineteenth-century houses and interesting courtyards and lanes leading from it. The nearby church has a fine fifteenth-century tower. The town once had two railway stations and it was famous for its fairs. Today it has a thriving printing works (established in 1864) and other light industries. There is an unusual gasworks museum opposite the disused watermill. Just outside Fakenham there is a racecourse. The Thursday market is worth a visit.

Museum of Gas and Local History, page 115.

In the locality: Warham Iron Age Fort, page 75; Creake Abbey, page 79; North Elmham Saxon Cathedral and Bishop's Castle, page 80; Walsingham Abbey, page 83; churches at Brisley, page 84; and Little Snoring, page 88; Walsingham Slipper Chapel, page 95; Houghton Hall, page 101; County School Station Museum, page 109; Thursford Museum, page 113; Shirehall Museum, page 113; Melton Constable Locomotive Works and Railway Housing, page 116; Great Bircham Windmill, page 120; Elmham Park Vineyards and Winery, page 126; Penthorpe Waterfowl Trust, page 128; Textile Centre, Great Walsingham, page 129. See also the

Walsinghams, page 52.

Felbrigg
Felbrigg Lakeside and Woodland Walks, page 57; Felbrigg Hall, page 100.

Filby
The ending -by in English place-names, found frequently in the Broads area, indicates a Danish origin. Filby Broad is one of the Trinity Broads and no longer navigable but the area is popular with naturalists and holidaymakers. The church of All Saints has medieval paintings, flushwork and an intriguing door to the belfry stairs with seven locks.
Filby Broad, page 64.

Fleggburgh
Bygone Village, page 125.

Foulden
Foulden Watermill, page 120.

Framingham Earl
Church of St Andrew, page 87.

Fritton
Fritton Decoy and Lake, page 66.

Garboldisham
Garboldisham Windmill, page 120.

Geldeston
This village is a reminder of the days when waterways were more important than roads. Geldeston village once had a staithe for trading wherries at the head of the navigable dyke that leads from the river Waveney. Today there is a boatyard and moorings for pleasure boats near the Wherry Inn. Further upstream is the used tidal lock near the Locks Inn. Geldeston also had a railway station, built to serve the Waveney Valley line, and there are the remains of the station, a brewery and maltings. There are some fine houses in the village, some enclosed with crinkle-crankle walls. The church and hall stand some distance from the present village. In the churchyard there are some interesting gravestones.
Geldeston Tidal Lock, page 115.

In the locality: churches at Hales, page 87; Loddon, page 88; and Shelton, page 94; Otter Trust, page 128.

Glandford
Glandford, a pretty village in the Glaven valley in north Norfolk, was rebuilt as a picturesque model village by the Jodrell family around 1900. The church was also reconstructed and is complete with rood and parclose screens, hammerbeam roof, marble font and carved pew ends.

Gooderstone
Church of St George, page 87; Gooderstone Water Gardens, page 100.

Gorleston-on-Sea
Early closing Wednesday.
Although much older than Great Yarmouth, this town is now a suburb of its neighbour on the opposite bank of the Yare but it has retained a character of its own. The beach is backed by low cliffs to form a bay, from which sailing dinghies operate. There is a lifeboat station and a ferry across the river on weekdays. Like Great Yarmouth it offers amusements for holidaymakers and a flat sandy beach with some pebbles. There are interesting nineteenth-century villas and a pavilion (1898) which serves as a theatre and dance hall in summer. The church of St Andrew has a fine fourteenth-century brass and the Roman Catholic church (1938) was designed by Eric Gill.
In the locality: see Great Yarmouth, below.

Great Bircham
Great Bircham Windmill, page 120.

Great Walsingham
See the Walsinghams, page 52.

Great Yarmouth
Early closing Thursday (six-day trading almost universal in the summer); market days Wednesday, Friday (summer only) and Saturday.
Great Yarmouth is above all a popular seaside resort and amusement arcades, souvenir shops, ice-cream parlours, restaurants and

Central Beach and Britannia Pier, Great Yarmouth.

night clubs abound. Two piers present summer shows and other attractions include an award-winning leisure centre, funfairs, bowling greens, a racecourse and a yachting station. There is a long sandy beach to the east of the town and other beaches to the north at Caister, Scratby, Hemsby and Winterton; these villages also have large caravan parks. Yarmouth Council employs beach guards to protect bathers. Cruises on the Broads and coach tours to the surrounding countryside are available in summer.

The town is built alongside the river Yare on a 3 mile (5 km) spit of sand which began to form in Roman times, and much of its wealth has been based on the port and rich herring fishery which developed. The fishery has declined but the port remains busy as a result of the North Sea oil and gas industry and trade from Europe. Great Yarmouth is vulnerable to flooding when winter high tides and gales coincide, as they did in 1953.

A good way to explore the historic part of the town is to walk round the ruins of the ancient walls built between 1261 and 1346, starting at the north-west tower near the White Swan Inn. The walk takes about an hour, and an illustrated leaflet describing the route is available from tourist information centres and museums. The wall passes close to St Nicho-

las's church, founded by Bishop Losinga, the Norman bishop of Norwich. It is one of the largest parish churches in England and was destroyed by fire in the Second World War and then rebuilt. Inside there is a modern stained glass window showing steam drifters, sailing boats, a wherry and the fishermen of Galilee. On the nearby Church Plain is the fine eighteenth-century vicarage, and next door an older house where Anna Sewell, the author of *Black Beauty*, was born (see page 135). Across the road near the market is the Fishermen's Hospital (1702), with oval inscription boards detailing the rules to be followed by inmates. The walk passes by Alexandra Road and King Street, where there are interesting houses of the eighteenth and nineteenth centuries, built as boarding houses when Yarmouth first became a genteel seaside resort.

Much of old Yarmouth was destroyed during bombing raids in the Second World War, especially in the Rows, the narrow alleyways running across the spit of land that forms the town. These are unique to Yarmouth. One of the few remaining Rows (Row 111) is now cared for by English Heritage. Other important buildings are the eighteenth-century St George's church, now an arts centre, and the fine sequence of houses on South Quay, two

of which are now museums. Also in South
Quay are Greyfriars Cloisters. Yarmouth has
historic links with Lord Nelson (see page
132) and there is a monument 144 feet (44
metres) high to him on South Denes. There is
a viewing platform on top, reached by an
internal staircase.

North Denes Beach Little Tern Colony,
page 59; **Greyfriars' Cloisters**, page 79; **Old
Merchant's House and Row 111 Houses**,
page 101; **Elizabethan House Museum**, page
106; **Lydia Eva Steam Drifter**, page 106;
Maritime Museum for East Anglia, page
106; **Tolhouse Museum and Brass Rubbing Centre**, page 106; **Kingdom of the Sea**,
page 126.

*In the locality: the Broads, chapter 4, page
64; Weavers' Way, pages 62 and 71; Burgh
Castle, page 74; Caister-on-Sea Roman
Town, page 74; Caister Castle, page 78;
Reedham Ferry, page 117; Berney Arms High
Mill, page 118; Thrigby Corn Mill, page 123;
Stracey Arms Windpump, page 123; Thrigby
Hall Wildlife Gardens, page 129. See also
Acle, page 15.*

Gressenhall
Norfolk Rural Life Museum, page 107.

Gunton
Near Cromer.
Gunton Sawmill, page 116.

Haddiscoe
Haddiscoe is surrounded by marshland and in
Roman times it was part of a large estuary
that extended up the Waveney valley as far as
Beccles. The church of St Mary and part of
the village stand on higher ground overlook-
ing the marshes. The church has a chequered
cap to its round tower and there is a remark-
able Norman carving above the south door.
Look also for the monument to the wife of the
Dutchman Jan Piers, the 'Master of the
Dykes', who helped drain the Haddiscoe
Marshes.
Haddiscoe Marshes, page 66.

Hales
Church of St Margaret, page 87; Hales Hall
and Gardens, page 100.

Happisburgh
A red and white banded lighthouse and a tall
church tower dominate the skyline of this
popular seaside village (pronounced 'Haze-
bro'), both valuable landmarks for mariners.
12 miles (19 km) off the shore lie the treacherous Happisburgh Sands, the cause of many
shipwrecks. The beach here has been praised
in a European Community report on English
beaches. The village has many interesting
flint houses and thatched cottages, including
the sixteenth-century Monastery Cottage.
Near the lighthouse is St Mary's Hotel, formerly Happisburgh Manor (1900, by Detmar
Blow), with interesting brickwork in the art
nouveau style.
Church of St Mary, page 87.

*In the locality: the Broads, chapter 4, page
64; Broomholm Priory, page 77; churches at
North Walsham, page 88; Trunch, page 94;
Worstead, page 97; North Walsham to Dilham
Canal, page 116. See also Aylsham, page
15; North Walsham, page 32; Stalham, page
49.*

Harleston
*Early closing Thursday; market day
Wednesday.*
This small town in south Norfolk, now bypassed by the A143, has many fine Georgian
houses and a handsome William and Mary
house called Candlers. The clock-tower and
the seventeenth-century Magpie Inn in the
market square are very attractive and in the
Old Market Place there are courtyards where
weavers and basketmakers once lived.
*In the locality: New Buckenham Castle,
page 79; churches at Pulham St Mary, page
90; Shelton, page 94; and South Lopham,
page 94; Bressingham Gardens and Live
Steam Museum, pages 99 and 104; 100th
Bomb Group Memorial Museum, page 112;
Billingford Windmill, page 118; Starston
Windpump, page 122; Banham Zoo, page
125; Cranes Watering Farm, page 126; Otter
Trust, page 128; Pulham Market Vineyard,
page 129. See also Diss, page 21.*

Heacham
The village sign at Heacham recalls the Red
Indian princess Pocahontas, whom John Rolfe

of Heacham Hall married and brought to England in 1616. There is another monument to her in the church of St Mary. Heacham is situated just to the south of Hunstanton and it has grown rapidly in recent times. On the outskirts of the village there is a carrstone watermill but it is a lavender mill which now dominates and perfumes the village in the summer. Norfolk Lavender is famous all over the world and the sight of 100 acres (40 hectares) of lavender of various shades in bloom is worth seeing.

Norfolk Lavender, page 127.

In the locality: see Hunstanton, page 29.

Hickling

The beautiful reed-fringed Broad and its boating facilities dominate this attractive village, which is surrounded by coastal and Broadland nature reserves and walks. The tower of St Mary's church can be seen for miles across the marshes and the nearby coastal dunes. On the road to Sea Palling the remains of an Augustinian priory can be seen among the farm buildings. Sea Palling and nearby Horsey are situated on the exposed stretch of coast which suffered in the 1953 floods. There are plans for a prestigious Broads Museum to be established in disused boatyards at Hickling.

Hickling National Nature Reserve, page 66.

In the locality: Horsey, page 58; Winterton Dunes National Nature Reserve, page 63; Filby Broad, page 64; Horsey Mere, page 66; How Hill, pages 67 and 121; Martham Broad Nature Reserve, page 70; Ormesby Broad, page 70; Ranworth Broad and Conservation Centre, page 70; St Benet's Abbey, page 81; churches at Happisburgh, page 87; Ranworth, page 91; Tunstead, page 95; and Worstead, page 97; Potter Heigham medieval bridge, page 117; Horsey Windpump, page 121; St Benet's Abbey Mill, page 122; Thrigby Corn Mill, page 123; Thurne Dyke Windpump, page 123; Thrigby Hall Wildlife Gardens, page 129; Wroxham Barns, page 129. See also Potter Heigham, page 42; Stalham, page 49; and Wroxham, page 54.

Hingham

Early closing Wednesday.

Abraham Lincoln's ancestors came from Hingham and sailed to religious freedom in North America in 1637. It is a most attractive town with elegant eighteenth-century houses surrounding two open greens. It also has a fine church.

Church of St Andrew, page 87.

In the locality: Thompson Common, page 62; Wayland Wood, page 62; Wymondham Abbey, page 83; church at Attleborough, page 84; Industrial Steam Museum, page 105; Wymondham Heritage Museum, page 114; Caston Windmill, page 119. See also Watton, page 53; and Wymondham, page 55.

Holkham

Holkham Lake Walk and Farm Walk, page 57; Holkham National Nature Reserve, page 57; Holkham Hall and Gardens, page 100; Bygones at Holkham, page 107.

Holt

Early closing Thursday.

Holt is a compact small town which is full of interest. It was practically destroyed by fire in

Milepost, Holt.

The river Bure at Horning.

1708 and rebuilt on the medieval street plan around the Market Place. On Fish Hill crowded market stalls became house sites after the fire and this area now forms a fascinating island of shops. There are elegant eighteenth-century houses, Victorian terraces, flint cottages and yards where there were once workshops for craftsmen. The large Victorian house on the east side of the Market Place stands on the site of the manor house where Sir John Gresham started a grammar school in 1555 – now Gresham's School. The house is still used by the school but the main school building is now just outside the town on the Cromer road. The town has become a high-class residential area with many speciality shops and pleasant countryside nearby.

Holt Lowes Country Park, page 58.

In the locality: Felbrigg Lakeside and Woodland Walks, page 57; Kelling Heath Nature Trail, page 58; Mannington Walks, page 58; Roman Camp and Beeston Regis Heath, page 60; Wiveton Downs Picnic Area, page 63; Baconsthorpe Castle, page 77; Walsingham Abbey, page 83; churches at Blakeney, page 84; and Cley, page 85; Felbrigg Hall, page 100; Mannington Gardens and Countryside, page 101; Wolterton Hall Gardens, page 103; Letheringsett Watermill, page 121; Textile Centre, page 129. See

also Blakeney, page 16; Cley-next-the-Sea, page 20; and the Walsinghams, page 52.

Horning

Early closing Wednesday.

This Broads holiday village stretches for about a mile along the river Bure. The Edwardian lodges and thatched cottages mingle with modern houses, shops, restaurants, pubs and boathouses along the waterfront and main street. A regatta is held every August and the Three Rivers Race starts here every June. There are interesting walks in and around the village. Horning church has carved bench ends and the ruined St Benet's Abbey is close by.

St Benet's Abbey, page 81; **St Benet's Abbey Mill**, page 122.

In the locality: Barton Broad, page 64; Belaugh, page 64; Cockshoot Broad, page 64; How Hill, pages 67 and 121; Ranworth Broad and Conservation Centre, page 70; Salhouse Broad, page 70; Womack Water, page 71; Wroxham Broad, page 73; churches at Ludham, page 88; Ranworth, page 91; and Tunstead, page 95; Beeston Hall and Gardens, page 98; Fairhaven Garden Trust, page 99; Bygone Village, page 125; Redwings Horse Sanctuary, page 129; Wroxham Barns, page 129. See also Coltishall, page 20;

Stalham, page 49; Wroxham, page 54.

Horsey

Horsey Nature Reserve, page 58; Horsey Mere, page 66; Horsey Windpump, page 121.

Houghton

Houghton Hall, page 101.

Houghton St Giles

Walsingham Slipper Chapel, page 95.

Hoveton

Hoveton lies alongside Wroxham Broad at the very centre of Broadland. The boundary between Hoveton and Wroxham runs along the centre of the river and much of what is popularly known as Wroxham, including the railway station, a number of boatyards and Roys large store, are in fact in Hoveton.

Hoveton Great Broad Nature Trail, page 67; **Hoveton Hall Gardens**, page 101.

In the locality: see Wroxham, page 54.

Hunstanton

Early closing Thursday; market day Wednesday.

The ornate Victorian and Edwardian houses around the spacious greens and along the seafront were built during the heyday of the town (called 'Hunston' by older Norfolk people) after the coming of the railway, which linked the east coast with the Midlands. The railway closed in 1969 but visitors still come by car and coach. Hunstanton has a lot to offer as a seaside resort: good sands, plentiful amusements, shops, well-tended gardens, a golf course and a delightful walk along the top of the famous striped cliffs to the lighthouse. This is the only west-facing resort on the east coast and so the visitor can watch the sun set over the Wash.

Kingdom of the Sea, page 126.

In the locality: Brancaster Manor Recreation Area, page 56; Ringstead Downs, page 60; Sandringham Country Park, page 61; Snettisham Nature Reserve, page 61; Scolt Head Island National Nature Reserve, page 61; Titchwell Marsh Nature Reserve, page 62; Brancaster Roman Fort, page 74; Burn-ham Norton Friary, page 78; Castle Rising Castle, page 78; Creake Abbey, page 79; churches at the Burnhams, page 84; Walsingham Slipper Chapel, page 95; Sandringham House, Grounds and Museum, page 102; Forge Museum, page 109; Shirehall Museum, page 113; Wells and Walsingham Light Railway, page 117; Great Bircham Windmill, page 120; Snettisham Watermill, page 122; Congham Hall Herb Garden, page 125; Courtyard Farm, page 125; Park Farm, page 128.

Kelling

Kelling Heath Nature Trail, page 58.

King's Lynn

Early closing Wednesday; market days Tuesday and Saturday.

King's Lynn grew rapidly after the Second World War when it became an overspill town for London. It was suddenly swamped with new estates and there was much over-hasty demolition and redevelopment. Now it seems to be recovering its poise and its reputation as a handsome historic town. The town stands on the river Great Ouse on the shores of the Wash and is growing in importance as a port. From the thirteenth century the Hanseatic League countries were Lynn's main trading partners and Baltic ships are still frequent visitors. The busy modern docks are tucked away behind security fences to the north of the town and there are industrial estates there and to the south.

Lynn (it was Bishop's Lynn until the King seized it in 1536) has had many admirers: Pevsner called it 'delightful', John Seymour called it 'England's most romantic town', and Defoe in the eighteenth century thought it had 'gentry and gaiety'. If you visit the festival week in July you would agree with Defoe but in Mart Week in February, when a funfair invades the Tuesday Market, you would find more robust pleasures.

King's Lynn is a compact town and easily explored on foot. Start at the Saturday Market Place near the beautiful St Margaret's church, which faces Trinity Guildhall (1421), with its amazing chequered stone front. Used originally for guild feasts and meetings, it is now the town hall and tourist information centre.

The undercroft houses the town's important collection of regalia and a museum of punishments. Nearby is a museum of town life with a re-created Victorian garden. The Saturday Market was the centre of the first medieval town and close by in St Margaret's Lane is a Hanseatic warehouse.

Walk down the narrow, winding Queen Street: on the left is Thoresby College (1508), built for priests attached to the Trinity Guild. The houses on this side of the street back on to the river; they were merchants' houses, each with a staithe and warehouse, many of which are today being converted into residences. Clifton House in Queen Street is noteworthy, with its portico with twisted pillars. Cross the Purfleet to what in the twelfth century was 'newland' and to the second medieval town, which had its own market, fair and fortifications. Turn into King Street, wider than Queen Street and with similar wealthy merchants' houses. The Custom House (1683) has a statue to Charles I over the doorway, a reminder that Lynn supported the royal cause in the Civil War. The father of one of the town's heroes, George Vancouver (see page 133), was a cus-

Red Mount Chapel, King's Lynn.

toms officer here. His son sailed with Captain Cook and later acquired British Columbia for the British. Among the fine houses in King Street, Number 9 and Numbers 30 and 32 (now a solicitors' office) are particularly noteworthy. St George's Guildhall at the far end is owned by the National Trust and used as the Fermoy Centre.

Walk through to the riverside restaurant before continuing into the Tuesday Market. Originally the market square was open to the river to the north and west and streets led to Fisher Fleet, still the fishermen's quarter. From the market St Nicholas Street leads to the beautiful St Nicholas's Chapel. Make your way to Chapel Street, past the fifteenth-century Lattice House, and to Austin Street, where there are the remains of an Augustinian friary. Continue through to the bus station and the town museum. Cross the busy St James Road to St James Park and the Red Mount Chapel and to Greyfriars' Tower, on the other side of London Road, in its own park. St James Street will bring you back to the Saturday Market. There is plenty more to see: the South Gate, the remains of the town walls, the Jacobean Greenland Fisheries Building and Hampton Court are worth a visit.

Greyfriars' Tower, page 79; **church of St Margaret**, page 87; **Medieval Merchant's House**, page 101; **St George's Guildhall**, page 102; **Fermoy Centre**, page 107; **Lynn Museum**, page 107; **Old Gaol House Museum, Regalia Rooms and Heritage Centre**, page 108; **Town House Museum of Lynn Life**, page 108; **True's Yard**, page 108; **Caithness Crystal**, page 125.

In the locality: Roydon Common, page 60; Sandringham Country Park, page 61; Castle Rising Castle, page 78; churches at Terrington St Clement, page 94; Tilney All Saints, page 94; Walpole St Peter, page 95; Wiggenhall St Mary the Virgin, page 95; Sandringham House, page 102; Congham Hall Herb Garden, page 125; Norfolk Lavender, page 127.

Langham
Langham Glass, page 127.

Langley
Langley Dyke and Staithe, page 67.

Letheringsett
Letheringsett Watermill, page 121.

Little Cressingham
Little Cressingham Wind and Water Mill, page 121.

Little Snoring
Church of St Andrew, page 88.

Little Walsingham
See the Walsinghams, page 52.

Loddon
Early closing Wednesday.
This is an increasingly popular boating centre on the river Chet with access to the Broads. The town and neighbouring Chedgrave have many new housing estates, including a much admired group of council houses by the architects Tayler and Green. A fine church overlooks the green, and there are Georgian and Victorian houses along the main street, and warehouses and an old watermill from the days when Loddon was a commercial port.
Church of the Holy Trinity, page 88; **Loddon Watermill**, page 121.
In the locality: the Broads, chapter 4, page 64; Hardley Flood, page 66; Langley Dyke and Staithe, page 67; church at Hales, page 87; Hales Hall and Gardens, page 100; Raveningham Gardens, page 102; Geldeston Tidal Lock, page 115; Reedham Ferry, page 117; Pettitts Animal Adventure Park, page 129.

The Lophams
North and South Lopham were once important centres of the linen industry in south Norfolk and the prosperity it brought is evidenced by the fine houses in the villages. In the 1830s there were no fewer than fifty weavers working in the area, using fine thread spun locally from the hemp grown here. It was the linen weavers who gave the bells and the east window to North Lopham church and the fine stained glass windows in the Lady Chapel to South Lopham church. The villages have some curious 'wonders' including a self-grown stile and a ford where two rivers rise –

the Ouse and the Waveney.
The fen at South Lopham is part of Suffolk Wildlife's Redgrave and South Lopham Fen reserve, famous for the great raft spider.
Church of St Andrew, South Lopham, page 94.
In the locality: New Buckenham Castle, page 79; churches at East Harling, page 86; Pulham St Mary, page 90; and Wilby, page 97; Bressingham Gardens, page 99; Bressingham Live Steam Museum, page 104; Diss Museum, page 105; 100th Bomb Group Memorial Museum, page 112; Billingford Windmill, page 118; Garboldisham Windmill, page 120; Cranes Watering Farm, Starston, page 126. See also Attleborough, page 15; Diss, page 21; and Harleston, page 26.

Ludham
Ludham is one of the most attractive Broads villages. It stands on slightly higher ground between the rivers Thurne, Bure and Ant and is connected by the Thurne to Womack Water, which has facilities for boating. There is a pretty cluster of eighteenth-century houses, many thatched, around the church, with a village store, teashops and craft shops. Nearby are the ruins of St Benet's Abbey and How Hill, and the skyline is dotted with windpumps.
Church of St Catherine, page 88.
In the locality: Barton Broad, page 64; Cockshoot Broad, page 64; Hickling Broad National Nature Reserve, page 66; Horsey Mere, page 66; How Hill, pages 67 and 121; South Walsham Broad, page 70; Sutton Broad, page 71; Upton Fen, page 71; Womack Water, page 71; Wroxham Broad, page 73; St Benet's Abbey, page 81; churches at Ranworth, page 91; South Burlingham, page 94; and Tunstead, page 95; Beeston Hall and Gardens, page 98; Fairhaven Garden Trust, page 99; Hoveton Hall Gardens, page 101; Horsey Windpump, page 121; St Benet's Abbey Mill, page 122; Sutton Windmill, page 123; Bygone Village, page 125; Wroxham Barns, page 129.

Mannington
Mannington Walks, page 58; Mannington Gardens and Countryside, page 101.

Martham

Martham Broad Nature Reserve, page 70.

Melton Constable

Locomotive Works and Railway Housing, page 116.

Morston

Morston and Stiffkey Marshes, page 58.

Mundesley

There are smooth sandy beaches and plenty of facilities for visitors at this quiet seaside resort built at the mouth of the tiny river Mund. The town prospered at the beginning of the twentieth century, when there was a railway here, and there are some fine houses and hotels dating from this era. For a time Mundesley was something of a health resort with two sanatoriums for consumptive patients attracted by the bracing sea breezes. **Stow High Windmill,** page 123.

In the locality: Blickling Park Walks, page 56; Felbrigg Lakeside and Woodland Walks, page 57; Broomholm Priory, page 77; churches at Happisburgh, page 87; North Walsham, page 88; and Trunch, page 94; Alby Gardens, page 98; Blickling Hall, page 98; Felbrigg Hall, page 100; Wolterton Hall Gardens, page 103; Gunton Sawmill, page 116; Alby Craft Centre, page125.

Narborough

There are bronze age, iron age and Roman remains at Narborough on the river Nar, now overgrown but once navigable. The old maltings and the Ship Inn are relics of that time. The village is now bypassed by the A47 and becoming a popular residential village with a new school and a community centre. **Narborough Railway Line**, page 59; **Narborough Watermill**, page 122.

New Buckenham

See the Buckenhams, page 18.

North Creake

Creake Abbey, page 79; Forge Museum, page 109.

North Elmham

The road from East Dereham to Fakenham winds through this pretty village, which has many interesting features, including the site of the 'Saxon' Cathedral, a fine church, Nelson House, where a relative of Lord Nelson once lived, the Elmham Park Vineyard and a museum in a restored railway station. **Saxon Cathedral and Bishop's Castle,** page 80; **church of St Mary the Virgin,** page 88; **County School Station Museum,** page 109; **Elmham Park Vineyards and Winery,** page 126.

North Lopham

See the Lophams, page 31.

North Walsham

Early closing Wednesday; market day Thursday.

The wool trade brought prosperity to North Walsham in the late middle ages and it has remained an important rural centre ever since. It suffered a great fire in 1600 and as a result most of the buildings are Georgian or Victorian, built during the period of development that followed the opening of the North Walsham to Dilham canal and the coming of the railway. Today North Walsham is growing fast as a residential area and a centre for light industries. The centre of the town is little changed; there is a market cross (1550), alleyways and interesting shops to explore and the church of St Nicholas just off the market square. **Church of St Nicholas**, page 88; **North Walsham to Dilham Canal**, page 116.

In the locality: Bacton Wood Forest Trail, page 56; Blickling Park Walks, page 56; Felbrigg Lakeside and Woodland Walks, page 57; Broomholm Priory, page 77; churches at Happisburgh, page 87; and Trunch, page 94; Alby Gardens, page 98; Blickling Hall, page 98; Felbrigg Hall, page 100; Wolterton Hall Gardens, page 103; Gunton Sawmill, page 116; Alby Craft Centre, page 125.

Norwich

Early closing Thursday; provisions market weekdays.

Norwich is a proud city and rightly so. George

Opposite: Elm Hill, Norwich.

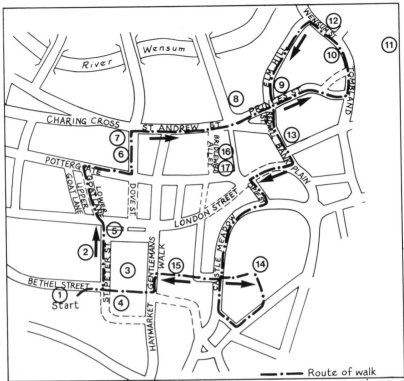

Norwich city centre: 1 Central Library, 2 City Hall, 3 Market, 4 St Peter Mancroft, 5 Guildhall, 6 Maddermarket Theatre, 7 Strangers' Hall Museum, 8 St Andrew's and Blackfriars' Halls, 9 St Peter Hungate Church Museum, 10 Augustine Steward's House, 11 Cathedral, 12 Maid's Head Hotel, 13 St Michael-at-Plea, 14 Castle Museum, 15 Royal Arcade, 16 Bridewell Museum, 17 The Mustard Shop.

Borrow said it was 'a fine old city, truly – view it from whatever side you will', and Nikolaus Pevsner wrote: 'Only the city of London and York can compare with Norwich in density of interesting buildings and intricacy of street pattern.' It has been called the city of churches; at one time there were more than fifty and there are still 33 medieval churches, although many are no longer used for worship. There are a thousand listed buildings, many of the eighteenth century, and many fine examples of modern architecture. In recent times Norwich has had the distinction of being the only English city to be included in a list of European Community cities which are prosperous but yet preserve social amenities. It still has the atmosphere of a large market town and you will hear plenty of Norfolk voices in the streets.

Guided tours

There are tours of the city leaving from the tourist information centre at the Guildhall on weekdays in summer, with a special theme tour on Sundays.

'Norwich Discovery', a series of illustrated leaflets published by the Norwich City Council, describes in detail walks in the city centre on various themes. The walk described below is for those with less time and can be undertaken in a morning.

A walk around the city centre

The walk begins at the car park near the Central Library, a distinctive modern building with panels of dressed flint. The nearby

City Hall is considered to be one of the best municipal buildings of the 1930s. Below it is a large open-air market with colourful stalls spilling out on to the pavements, giving the city a continental air. Looking down on the market is St Peter Mancroft church, and below it is a group of seventeenth-century and eighteenth-century houses, including the Sir Garnet Wolseley public house, which the Norwich Society has listed as the best Norwich pub. On the other side of the market is the fifteenth-century Guildhall with its magnificent chequer pattern of flint and stone on the east end. It is now the tourist information centre.

From the Guildhall walk down one of the narrow streets leading towards the river – Dove Street or Lower or Upper Goat Lane, each with its speciality shops. You will arrive in Pottergate, originally the potters' quarter; walk towards St John Maddermarket church and through an arch to the Maddermarket Theatre, an Elizabethan-style theatre which has been the home of the Norwich Players since 1921. It is usually open and visitors are welcome. The Maddermarket was the place where madder, a valuable red dye, was sold when Norwich was an important centre of the woollen industry. The street below the theatre is known as Charing Cross ('shearing cross'); here is the Strangers' Hall Museum. Across the road to the right is a multi-storey

The Guildhall, Norwich.

Cobbled streets near Elm Hill, Norwich.

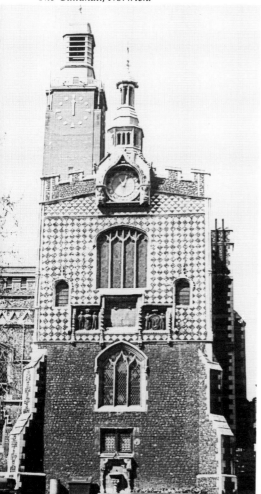

Cliffs at Cromer.   Opposite: *Thetford Warren.*

Harvest time in north Norfolk with the Forestry Commission's Wensum Forest in the background.

car park on the site of the former palace of the Dukes of Norfolk (see page 138), demolished by the Duke in 1711 in a fit of pique. Turn right to St Andrew's Street. Across the road on the left are St Andrew's Hall and Black-friars' Hall, now used for public meetings, concerts and craft and antique fairs. Opposite the halls is St Andrew's church. Turn into Princes Street which leads to St Peter Hungate church, now a church museum. At the lower end of Princes Street is Tombland ('empty land'), the site of the first market place and now a pleasant cobbled square. Look for Augustine Steward's House. Opposite is the cathedral. Walk towards the river along Wensum Street past the Maid's Head Hotel, an historic coaching inn, and turn right up Elm Hill. This cobbled street, with its mixture of architectural styles from medieval to Victorian, is one of the most picturesque in Norwich. The street narrowly escaped demolition in the 1930s and now has interesting speciality shops. At the far end is the Briton's Arms, a thatched fifteenth-century house. It was once the home of craft workers and has also been a religious house and an inn; now it is a restaurant.

Turn left up the hill to Redwell Street and Bank Plain. On the left is the church of St

Norwich Castle and Castle Mall.

Michael-at-Plea, now an antique centre. Turn right into London Street, a pedestrian precinct which lives up to its name by having branches of many prestigious London stores.

After exploring London Street turn up Opie Street to Castle Meadow, cross the road and climb the steps to the Norman castle, now a museum. Below the castle to the south is the new Castle Mall, with shops, roof gardens and an underground car park.

Walk through Castle Gardens (notice the sculpture by Barbara Hepworth) and cross to the Back of the Inns, originally the course of a stream or 'cockey' and the site of yards, stables and servants' quarters behind the many inns that stood here. Walk through the Royal Arcade on the left, a brilliant example of art nouveau architecture. It leads back to the market and Gentleman's Walk, which was 'clubland' to the young bloods of the city in the eighteenth century. Turn left to the Haymarket, where the statue of Sir Thomas Browne (see page 135) looks down (the relics and a memorial tablet to this seventeenth-century writer may be seen in St Peter Mancroft church nearby). Walk past the church back to the car park.

There are many other areas to explore, such

Pull's Ferry, Norwich.

as the cathedral area and Bridewell Alley, which has the Bridewell Museum, the Mustard Shop and a famous basket shop: and 'across the water' there is Colegate, another fascinating area.

The river Wensum

The Wensum is not a large river but it is just wide enough and deep enough to be navigable from the sea, and for Norwich to be a port and a yacht station. There is a waymarked riverside walk from Carrow Bridge up river to the New Mills, with information panels displayed along the way.

Water cruises through the city to the Broads operate daily in summer, subject to winds and tides. The boats are covered, refreshments are available on board and a commentary is provided. Details from Southern River Steamers, 43 Ebbisham Drive, Norwich NR4 6HQ. Telephone: 0603 501220.

Yare Valley Walk, page 63; **Norwich Castle**, page 80; **Norwich Cathedral Cloisters,** page 80; **St Andrew's and Blackfriars' Halls**, page 81; **Norwich Cathedral**, page 88; **Friends' Meeting House**, page 89; **church of St Peter Mancroft**, page 90; **churches of St Mary Coslany** and **St Michael at Coslany**, page 90; **Octagon Chapel**, page 90; **Old Meeting House**, page 90; **Roman Catholic Cathedral**, page 90; **church of St Julian**, page 90; **Augustine Steward's House**, page 98; **City of Norwich Aviation Museum**, page 109; **Bridewell Museum of Norwich Trades and Industries**, page 109; **Castle Museum**, page 109; **Norwich Gallery**, page 109; **City Regalia**, page 109; **Norwich Arts Centre**, page 109; **Royal Norfolk Regimental Museum**, page 110; **Sainsbury Centre for Visual Arts**, page 110; **St Peter Hungate Church Museum**, page 110; **Strangers' Hall Museum**, page 110.

In the locality: Surlingham Church Marsh, page 70; Whitlingham Country Park, page 71; Arminghall Henge Monument, page 74; Caistor St Edmund Roman Town, page 74; St Faith's Priory, page 82; church at Framingham Earl, page 87. See also Thorpe St Andrew, page 51.

Old Buckenham
See the Buckenhams, page 18.

Ormesby
Ormesby Broad, page 70.

Wild flowers by a Norfolk lane in July.

Cultivated lavender at the Norfolk Lavender Centre, Heacham.

Reedham chain ferry.

Cockley Cley Iceni Village.

Overstrand

Below the crumbling cliffs at Overstrand lies the earlier fishing village of Beckhythe; now parts of Overstrand are vulnerable to cliff falls. For the first three decades of the twentieth century Overstrand was known as 'the village of millionaires': the rich and famous came here, attracted by Clement Scott's romantic writings about 'Poppyland'. Many beautiful houses date from this period, including The Pleasaunce by Lutyens, which had a garden designed by Gertrude Jekyll, and Pear Tree Cottage, a large house (now divided), which was owned by Lord Randolph Churchill, the father of Sir Winston Churchill. It is still a popular seaside place, in spite of the sea defences that dominate the beaches. Look for fossils in the cliffs.

Poppyland, page 59; **The Pleasaunce**, page 102.

In the locality: Felbrigg Lakeside and Woodland Walks, page 57; Roman Camp and Beeston Regis Heath, page 60; West Runton Cliffs and Beach, page 63; churches at Cromer, page 86; and Trunch, page 94; Alby Gardens, page 98; Felbrigg Hall, page 100; Cromer Museum, page 104; Old Boathouse Lifeboat Museum, page 104; Gunton Sawmill, page 116; North Norfolk Railway, page 116; Northrepps Iron Foundry and Sawpit, page 116; Stow High Windmill, page 123; Alby Craft Centre, page 125. See also Cromer, page 20; Mundesley, page 32; Paston, below; Sheringham, page 47.

Paston

This north Norfolk village 1 mile (1.6 km) from the sea was the original home of the Paston family, prominent landowners and wool merchants in the middle ages and Tudor times. The Paston Letters (see page 136), written in the fifteenth century, give a vivid picture of contemporary life. The fine thatched tithe barn, one of the largest in Norfolk, was built in 1581. The thatched church of St Margaret contains interesting wall paintings and memorials, one of them with an inscription said to have been written by John Donne.

Potter Heigham
Early closing Wednesday.

Yachts and cruisers tie up at the moorings at the boatyards and riverside hotels of this busy Broads village. The interesting medieval bridge has carried the traffic over the river Thurne for seven hundred years but a new road bridge has now been built on the site of the old railway bridge. The true village is about a mile north of the somewhat untidy development along the river between the bridges. The name of the village is thought to derive from the days when the Romans had a pottery here.

Medieval Bridge, page 117.

In the locality: the Broads, chapter 4, page 64; Caister-on-Sea Roman Town, page 74; churches at Tunstead, page 95; and Worstead, page 97; Elizabethan House Museum, page 106; Lydia Eva Steam Drifter, page 106; Maritime Museum for East Anglia, page 106; Tolhouse Museum and Brass Rubbing Centre, page 106. See also Great Yarmouth, page 24; Wroxham, page 54.

The Pulhams

Pulham Market and the smaller Pulham St Mary are two attractive villages in the Waveney valley in south Norfolk. Many of the pretty colour-washed houses with steep roofs in Pulham Market date from more prosperous times in the sixteenth and seventeenth centuries. Manor Farm is a timber-framed house of about 1600. Pulham St Mary also has some outstanding early buildings: the fifteenth century church, and Pennoyer's School (1670), built into the Chapel of the Guild of St James (1401).

Church of St Mary the Virgin, page 90; **Pulham Market Vineyard**, page 129.

In the locality: New Buckenham Castle, page 79; churches at South Lopham, page 94; and Wilby, page 97; Bressingham Gardens and Live Steam Museum, pages 99 and 104; Burston Strike School Museum, page 104; 100th Bomb Group Memorial Museum, page 112; Billingford Windmill, page 118; Banham Zoo, page 125; Otter Trust, page 128. See also Attleborough, page 15; Diss, page 21; Harleston, page 26.

Ranworth
Ranworth Broad and Conservation

Centre, page 70; Church of St Mary, page 91.

Raveningham

Raveningham Gardens, page 102.

Reedham

This small village on the banks of the river Yare is very much a Broads boating centre. The river is deep here and strongly tidal. Reedham is also at one end of the New Cut linking the Waveney with the Yare. A chain ferry enables road traffic to cross. There is a railway station at Reedham which allows passengers from Norwich and Yarmouth to visit the nature reserves and windpumps via a footpath. Reedham has long been an important strategic river crossing – King Edmund had his headquarters here against the invading Danes. There is evidence of a church being founded here by St Felix in the seventh century on the site where the church of St John the Baptist stands today.

Reedham Ferry, page 117; **Berney Arms High Mill,** page 118; **Pettitts Animal Adventure Park,** page 129.

In the locality: Breydon Water Local Na-

Old Brewery House Hotel, Reepham.

ture Reserve, page 64; Haddiscoe Marshes, page 66; Hardley Flood, page 66; Langley Dyke and Staithe, page 67; Surlingham Church Marsh, page 70; Burgh Castle, page 74; churches at Hales, page 87; Loddon, page 88; and South Burlingham, page 94; Hales Hall and Gardens, page 100; Raveningham Gardens, page 102. See also Acle, page 15; Loddon, page 31; and Great Yarmouth, page 24.

Reepham

This is the town where Parson Woodforde (see page 136), the eighteenth-century diarist, did his shopping and it is still very much the centre for the farming community in the surrounding villages. The market square, near the three churches in one churchyard, has many fine eighteenth-century buildings, including Brewery House, now a hotel, with a sundial on the façade.

Church of St Mary, page 91; **Curiosity Street Experience,** page 126.

In the locality: Blickling Park Walks, page 56; Mannington Walks, page 58; North Elmham Saxon Cathedral and Bishop's Castle, page 80; churches at Booton, page 84; Brisley, page 84; Cawston, page 85; Elsing, page 87; North Elmham, page 88; and Salle, page 91; Blickling Hall, page 98; Mannington Gardens and Countryside, page 101; Norfolk Rural Life Museum, page 107; Elmham Park Vineyards and Winery, page 126; Norfolk Wildlife Park, page 128.

Ringstead

Ringstead Downs, page 60; Courtyard Farm, page 125.

Roydon

Roydon Common, page 60.

The Runtons

The many holidaymakers who stay at the caravan sites at East and West Runton enjoy the good beaches and the clifftop sites. The two villages have large commons with streams running through them and numerous cafés and seaside shops for the visitors. The north Norfolk coastal ridge here reaches its maximum height – 340 feet (104 metres), the high-

Thetford Priory.

Sandringham House.

est point in Norfolk. The cliffs and exposed rocks on parts of the beach are of great interest to geologists and fossil hunters. **West Runton Cliffs and Beach**, page 63; **Norfolk Shire Horse Centre**, page 128.

In the locality: Cley Marshes, page 56; Felbrigg Lakeside and Woodland Walks, page 57; Kelling Heath Nature Trail, page 58; Poppyland, page 59; Roman Camp and Beeston Regis Heath, page 60; Wiveton Downs Picnic Area, page 63; Baconsthorpe Castle, page 77; churches at Cley, page 85; and Cromer, page 86; Alby Gardens, page 98; Felbrigg Hall, page 100; Cromer Museum, page 104; Old Boathouse Lifeboat Museum, page 104; Cley Windmill, page 119; Letheringsett Watermill, page 121; Alby Craft Centre, page 125. See also Cley-next-the-Sea, page 20; Cromer, page 20; Holt, page 27; Sheringham, page 47.

St Olaves

St Olaves is a pretty village on the Waveney in the south of the county. It has boatyards, moorings and shops for provisioning boats and is the starting point of the New Cut, the canal dug in 1832 to connect the Waveney with the Yare and to provide Norwich with a direct route to the sea via Lowestoft and Oulton Broad, thus enabling it to be independent of Great Yarmouth. The plan was not a financial success but the Cut provides an alternative waterway for pleasure boats. Alongside the river and the Cut there are typical Broadland marshes rich in bird life and a footpath across the marshes starts at Haddiscoe Bridge. The church of St Mary has Norman features and a round tower with chequered decoration at the top. The numerous round-towered churches in this area are said to mark the old Saxon shore when the estuary from Great Yarmouth stretched far inland. There are ruins of an Augustinian priory (early thirteenth-century). **St Olaves Priory**, page 82; **St Olaves Windpump**, page 122.

In the locality: Berney Marshes, page 64; Haddiscoe Marshes, page 66; Fritton Decoy and Lake, page 66; Hardley Flood, page 66; church at Hales, page 87; Hales Hall and Gardens, page 100; Raveningham Gardens, *page 102; Reedham Ferry, page 117; Berney Arms High Mill, page 118; Loddon Watermill, page 121. See also Great Yarmouth, page 24.*

Salhouse

Salhouse Broad, page 70.

Salle

Church of St Peter and St Paul, page 91.

Salthouse

The Saxons gave this coastal village its name over a thousand years ago as 'a place for keeping salt'. The salt was obtained from sea water and used to preserve fish. Until the seventeenth century Salthouse had a quay but now there is just a trickle of water alongside the coast road with a few ducks where ships once sailed. There is graffiti representing ships on the backs of pews in the fifteenth-century church, probably the work of children when the church was used as a schoolroom. Today the village is popular with visitors for the scenery of the saltmarshes, the bird life and the samphire (edible glasswort) gathered here in the summer.

Salthouse Marsh Nature Reserve, Gramborough Hill and Walsey Hills Watchpoint, page 60.

In the locality: Blakeney Point, page 56; Cley Marshes, page 56; Felbrigg Lakeside and Woodland Walks, page 57; Holt Lowes Country Park, page 58; Kelling Heath Nature Trail, page 58; Morston and Stiffkey Marshes, page 58; Roman Camp and Beeston Regis Heath, page 60; West Runton Cliffs and Beach, page 63; Wiveton Downs Picnic Area, page 63; Baconsthorpe Castle, page 77; Felbrigg Hall, page 100; Sheringham Park, page 103; North Norfolk Railway, page 116; Cley Windmill, page 119; Letheringsett Watermill, page 121.

Sandringham

Sandringham Country Park, page 61; Sandringham House, Grounds and Museum, page 102.

Seething

Station 146, page 111.

Shelton

Church of St Mary, page 94.

Sheringham

*Early closing Wednesday; market day
Saturday.*

Today's town was once just a fishing settlement known as Sheringham Hythe, and Upper Sheringham further inland was the main village. Fishing and the coming of the railway in 1887 brought prosperity to Sheringham. At one time there were two hundred boats operating from the beach and the fishermen were able to send their catch to London by overnight train. Today fishing has declined but there are still a few commercial fishing boats. There are fishermen's cottages, some with net lofts, a lifeboat station and a tradition of knitting 'garnseys'. The railway also brought visitors, but the days when 64 trains arrived or departed (as in 1906) are long past although there is still a British Rail station and a steam railway, the North Norfolk Railway, which is mainly a tourist attraction and has a railway museum.

Sheringham has a good beach with rock pools at low tide, seaside amusements and a carnival in August. There is also a fine golf course – a true links course by the sea – and good walks in the surrounding countryside and at Sheringham Park.

Sheringham Park, page 103; **Railway Museum**, page 111; **Sheringham Museum**, page 111; **North Norfolk Railway**, page 116.

In the locality: Blakeney Point, page 56; Cley Marshes, page 56; Felbrigg Lakeside and Woodland Walks, page 57; Holt Lowes Country Park, page 58; Kelling Heath Nature Trail, page 58; Poppyland, page 59; Roman Camp and Beeston Regis Heath, page 60; West Runton Cliffs and Beach, page 63; Baconsthorpe Castle, page 77; churches at Blakeney, page 84; Cley, page 85; and Cromer, page 86; Felbrigg Hall, page 100; Cromer Museum, page 104; Old Boathouse Lifeboat Museum, page 104; Cley Windmill, page 119. See also Blakeney, page 16; Cley-next-the-Sea, page 20; Cromer, page 20; Holt, page 27.

Snettisham

Many of the older village houses at Snettisham

Restored shelter, Sheringham.

are built of the local carrstone, which is still quarried here. The village stands on the shores of the Wash and is famous for its bird sanctuary. It is also a popular holiday village. There are holiday chalets and a large caravan site alongside the marram-covered dunes and pebble beach.

Snettisham Nature Reserve, page 61; **Snettisham Watermill**, page 122; **Park Farm**, page 128.

South Burlingham

Church, page 94.

South Lopham

See the Lophams, page 31.

South Walsham

Two churches in a single churchyard, as in this village, are not uncommon in Norfolk. Only St Mary's at South Walsham is now in use as St Lawrence's was destroyed by fire in 1827 and only the ruins survive. A stream flows through the village: once it was navigable by wherries. A magnificent woodland garden was created by the Fairhaven family at South Walsham Hall and this is open to the

public. There is a 7 mile (11 km) circular waymarked walk to Upton, much of it alongside the river Bure.
South Walsham Broad, page 70; **Fairhaven Garden Trust**, page 99.

Stalham
Early closing Wednesday; market day Thursday.

This busy market town on the river Ant is a good centre from which to explore the northern section of the Broads, either by boat or by car. The staithe, once busy with the wherry trade, is on an artificial cut (or dyke) leading from the river and is separated from the town by the A149. The church of St Mary has one of the finest fifteenth-century fonts in England. The town is growing and has a busy shopping centre; the market is a good hunting ground for bric-à-brac as well as local produce.

In the locality: the Broads, chapter 4, page 64; Horsey, page 58; Hickling Broad National Nature Reserve, page 66; Horsey Mere, page 66; How Hill, pages 67 and 121; Broomholm Priory, page 77; churches at Happisburgh, page 87; Ludham, page 88; North Walsham, page 88; Trunch, page 94;

Swaffham.

Tunstead, page 95; and Worstead, page 97; Beeston Hall and Gardens, page 98; Hoveton Hall Gardens, page 101; North Walsham to Dilham Canal, page 116; Potter Heigham Medieval Bridge, page 117; Horsey Windpump, page 121; Stow High Windmill, page 123; Wroxham Barns, page 129. See also North Walsham, page 32; Wroxham, page 54.

Starston
Cranes Watering Farm, page 126; Starston Windpump, page 122.

Stiffkey
The flint and brick fishermen's cottages and small boarding houses cluster along the A149 coastal road, which here becomes a narrow winding street following the tiny river. The village is famous for its shellfish, especially the 'Stewky blues' – Stewky is the old pronunciation of Stiffkey. On the seaward side of the village there are saltmarshes and sand-dunes; inland there are farms and woodland. The church of St John stands alongside the ruins of an earlier church. Stiffkey achieved notoriety in the 1930s when its rector was unfrocked for associating with loose women and ended up

Opposite: *Sutton Windmill.*

being mauled to death by a tiger at Skegness Zoo. He is buried in the churchyard. **Morston and Stiffkey Marshes**, page 58. *For details of other places of interest in the locality, see Blakeney, page 16; Holt, page 27; Sheringham, page 47.*

Stoke Holy Cross

Stoke Holy Cross Watermill, page 123.

Strumpshaw

Strumpshaw Fen Nature Reserve, page 70; Strumpshaw Hall Steam Museum, page 111.

Surlingham

Surlingham Church Marsh, page 70.

Sutton

Sutton Broad, page 71; Sutton Windmill, page 123.

Swaffham

Early closing Thursday; market day Saturday.
This town stands at the centre of 'high' Norfolk, 210 feet (64 metres) above sea level, and far enough away from Norwich, King's Lynn and Thetford to acquire an importance of its own. In the eighteenth century it was the social centre for the local squires in winter and many of the town's handsome houses, the Assembly Rooms and the Coursing Club date from this time. The market cross was presented to the town by the Earl of Oxford in 1783. The market square is crowded with stalls on Saturdays and is a good place to look for bygones as well as local produce. At the north end of the market the town sign depicts the legendary Pedlar of Swaffham. He lived in Tudor times and was directed by a stranger he met in London to dig for treasure in his garden. He did so, found the treasure and in thanksgiving built the north aisle of the church. There is a museum.

Church of St Peter and St Paul, page 94; **Swaffham Museum**, page 112.

In the locality: Hoe Rough, page 57; Honeypot Wood Nature Reserve, page 58; Oxburgh Woodland Walk, page 59; Bichamditch, page 74; Castle Acre Bailey Gate, Castle and Priory, page 78; North Elmham Saxon Cathedral and Bishop's Castle, page 80; churches at Brisley, page 84; Castle Acre, page 85; East Dereham, page 86; Gooderstone, page 87;

The Charles Burrell Museum, Thetford.

North Elmham, page 88; and Oxborough, page 90; Gooderstone Water Gardens, page 100; Oxburgh Hall and Gardens, page 102; Norfolk Rural Life Museum, page 107; Caston Windmill, page 119; Little Cressingham Wind and Water Mill, page 121; Narborough Watermill, page 122; Cockley Cley Iceni Village and Museums, page 125; Elmham Park Vineyards and Winery, page 126.

Terrington St Clement

Church of St Clement, page 94.

Thetford

Early closing Wednesday; market days Tuesday and Saturday.

The fortunes of this, the largest town in Breckland, have waxed and waned through the centuries. It had a large Anglo-Saxon settlement in the ninth and tenth centuries, when it was briefly a cathedral town; in the thirteenth century there were thirteen parish churches in the town. Throughout the middle ages it remained an important monastic centre but after the Dissolution of the monasteries in the sixteenth century it became a sleepy country town. It was rudely awakened after the Second World War when it became an overspill town for London and its population quadrupled. Thetford acquired an industrial park and large new housing estates. The town centre has become a busy shopping centre and has been pedestrianised, space has been found for car parks, and sports facilities and an arts centre have been created. Much of old Thetford remains: old buildings of local chalk block and flint and Thetford grey brick, and open spaces by the river Thet. There is a castle mound (but no castle), a priory, and a museum. Thetford's most famous son was Thomas Paine (see page 131), born here in 1737, and one of the founding fathers of the American Revolution.

Thetford Forest Walks, page 61; **Thetford High Lodge Forest Centre,** page 61; **Thetford Priory**, page 82; **Thetford Warren Lodge**, page 103; **Ancient House Museum**, page 112; **Charles Burrell Museum**, page 112.

In the locality: East Wretham Heath, page 57; Weeting Heath, page 63; Grimes Graves, page 75; Weeting Castle, page 83; churches at East Harling, page 86; South Lopham, page 94; and Wilby, page 97; Bressingham Gardens and Live Steam Museum, pages 99 and 104; Garboldisham Windmill, page 120; Equine Rest and Rehabilitation Centres, page 126.

Thompson

Thompson Common, page 62.

Thornham

The sea once came up to the village, which had a natural harbour, but now it is a mile away across the saltmarshes. Many of the houses in the village are built of a mixture of local white and pink chalk as well as of flint and brick. The church of All Saints is partly Early English and partly Perpendicular and has good carved bench ends. Down Staithe Road across the marshes is the Lifeboat Inn, which, like the village itself, has a real Norfolk atmosphere.

In the locality: Brancaster Manor Recreation Area, page 56; Ringstead Downs, page 60; Scolt Head Island National Nature Reserve, page 61; Sandringham Country Park, page 61; Titchwell Marsh Nature Reserve, page 62; Brancaster Roman Fort, page 74; Castle Rising Castle, page 78; churches at the Burnhams, page 84; Houghton Hall, page 101; Sandringham House, Grounds and Museum, page 102; Great Bircham Windmill, page 120; Courtyard Farm, page 125. See also Hunstanton, page 29.

Thorpe St Andrew

The riverside scene at Thorpe, now a residential suburb of Norwich, was much painted by the Norwich School artists of the nineteenth century. Today it is a busy boating station on the 'old river' and no longer stands on the main waterway of the Yare. In 1844, when the railway was built, two bridges were constructed over the river and a 'cut' made so that river traffic could avoid them. The old reach is now used only by pleasure boats. Along the river front there are boatyards and moorings, restaurants and hotels. The imposing Thorpe Hall, which had fallen into disrepair, has been restored and can be seen from the river.

For details of places of interest in the locality, see Norwich, page 32.

Thrigby
Thrigby Corn Mill, page 123; Thrigby Hall Wildlife Gardens, page 129.

Thurne
Thurne Dyke Windpump, page 123.

Thursford
Thursford stands among the undulating cornlands of north Norfolk, halfway between Fakenham and Holt. The church has some of the finest Victorian church glass in England and some interesting monuments. **Thursford Wood**, page 62; **Thursford Museum**, page 113.

Tilney All Saints
All Saints Church, page 94.

Titchwell
Titchwell Marsh Nature Reserve, page 62.

Trunch
Church of St Botolph, page 94.

Tunstead
Church of St Mary, page 95.

Upton
Upton Fen, page 71.

Walpole
The two fenland villages of Walpole St Peter and Walpole St Andrew on the border between Norfolk and Lincolnshire have been amalgamated to form Walpole. It is here that King John's treasure is said to have been lost but all efforts have failed to locate it. One ancient treasure that survives is the church of St Peter, known as 'the Cathedral of the Fens'. **Church of St Peter**, page 95.

The Walsinghams
Little Walsingham is the place of pilgrimage; Great Walsingham is a most attractive village to the north-east. At Little Walsingham one steps back into the past and the atmosphere of a medieval pilgrimage town. Everywhere there are reminders of Walsingham's importance as one of Europe's great Christian shrines, where the Virgin Mary is reputed to have appeared. In the High Street a fifteenth-

Little Walsingham: the pump.

century gateway leads into the abbey grounds and to the ruins of the twelfth-century priory. There is a medieval pump in the cobbled square known as Common Place and an ancient guildhall, now a museum, in the Friday Market. This is still very much a pilgrimage centre, with many souvenir and craft shops. There is an Anglican shrine, a Roman Catholic pilgrim church, a Greek Orthodox church in the old railway station building and a Russian Orthodox church in a former chapel at Great Walsingham.

Walsingham Abbey, page 83; **Slipper Chapel**, page 95; **Shirehall Museum**, page 113; **Textile Centre**, page 129.

In the locality: Holkham National Nature Reserve, page 57; Morston and Stiffkey Marshes, page 58; Scolt Head Island National Nature Reserve, page 61; Thursford Wood, page 62; Warham Iron Age Fort, page 75; Binham Priory, page 77; Burnham Norton Friary, page 78; churches at Blakeney, page 84; the Burnhams, page 84; Cley, page 85; and Little Snoring, page 88; Holkham Hall and Gardens, page 100; Houghton Hall, page 101; Bygones at Holkham, page 107; Forge Museum, page 109; County School Station Museum, page 109; Wells and Walsingham Light Railway, page 117; Great Bircham Windmill, page 120; Langham Glass, page 127; Pensthorpe Waterfowl Trust, page 128.

Walsoken
Church of All Saints, page 95.

Warham
Warham Iron Age Fort, page 75.

Watton
Early closing Thursday; market day Wednesday.

Watton is a busy rural centre on the edge of Breckland, with an imposing clock tower (1679) in the High Street. It is an ancient town but a disastrous fire in 1674 destroyed sixty houses, so the buildings today are almost all of the eighteenth century or later. The town serves the farming community and personnel from the nearby air force base.

In the locality: East Wretham Heath, page 57; Oxburgh Woodland Walk, page 59; Thompson Common, page 62; Wayland Wood, page 62; Wymondham Abbey, page 83; churches at Attleborough, page 84; East Harling, page 86; Gooderstone, page 87; Hingham, page 87; Oxborough, page 90; Swaffham, page 94; and Wilby, page 97; Gooderstone Water Gardens, page 100; Oxburgh Hall and Gardens, page 102; Caston Windmill, page 119; Little Cressingham Wind and Water Mill, page 121; Wicklewood Windmill, page 124; Cockley Cley Iceni Village and Museums, page 125. See also Thetford, page 51.

Weeting
Weeting Heath, page 63; Weeting Castle, page 83.

Wells-next-the-Sea
Early closing Thursday; market day Wednesday (summer only).

Small cargo boats, pleasure craft and long-shore fishing boats (sprats and whelks are local specialities) tie up at the quay of this old-fashioned port. There are waterfront pubs, chandlery stores and a regatta and carnival in August, but unfortunately many of the old seafront buildings have been destroyed to make way for amusement arcades, burger bars and souvenir shops. Away from the seafront is Buttlands, a tree-fringed green surrounded by fine houses and once an archery practice ground. The Arts Centre is in a converted warehouse, and there is an Old Custom House in East Street. Seaside attractions include a wide beach known as Abraham's Bosom and a caravan park with amusements and sports facilities. A light railway operates to Walsingham during the summer.

Maritime Museum, page 113; **Wells and Walsingham Light Railway**, page 117.

In the locality: Blakeney Point, page 56; Cley Marshes, page 56; Holkham National Nature Reserve, page 57; Morston and Stiffkey Marshes, page 58; Thursford Wood, page 62; Warham Iron Age Fort, page 75; Binham Priory, page 77; Burnham Norton Friary, page 78; Walsingham Abbey, page 83; churches at Blakeney, page 84; Cley, page 85; and Little Snoring, page 88;

Walsingham Slipper Chapel, page 95; Holkham Hall and Gardens, page 100; Houghton Hall, page 101; Bygones at Holkham, page 107; Forge Museum, page 109; Thursford Museum, page 113; Shirehall Museum, page 113; Langham Glass, page 127; Textile Centre, page 129.

Welney
Welney Wildfowl Refuge, page 63.

West Runton
See the Runtons, page 43.

West Walton
Church of St Mary, page 95; Fenland Aviation Museum, page 113.

Weybourne
This coastal village nestles in a hollow with a beach running steeply to the sea. In the middle ages Weybourne had a market and there are still some remains of a thirteenth-century Augustinian priory. During both World Wars the village was of some military importance; the deep water of Weybourne Hope was used as an embarkation point in the First World War and in the Second the area was used for target practice by anti-aircraft guns. Now it is a quiet seaside resort with cobblestone cottages and winding streets. There is a cliff path to Sheringham.

Muckleburgh Collection, page 114.

In the locality: Blakeney Point, page 56; Cley Marshes, page 56; Felbrigg Lakeside and Woodland Walks, page 57; Kelling Heath Nature Trail, page 58; Roman Camp and Beeston Regis Heath, page 60; West Runton Cliffs and Beach, page 63; Wiveton Downs Picnic Area, page 63; Baconsthorpe Castle, page 77; churches at Blakeney, page 84; Cley, page 85; Felbrigg Hall, page 100; Sheringham Park, page 103; North Norfolk Railway, page 116; Cley Windmill, page 119; Letheringsett Watermill, page 121.

Wiveton
Wiveton Downs Picnic Area, page 63.

Wolferton
Wolferton Station Museum, page 114.

Wolterton
Wolterton Hall Gardens, page 103.

Worstead
The well-endowed church and the interesting houses that cluster round it are all that remains to show that this was once an important wool-weaving centre that gave its name to a type of woollen cloth. There are still buildings with large windows designed to give the weavers the maximum light. A festival is held here each year in July. At the edge of the village is Meeting Hill, an early nineteenth-century nonconformist settlement with a church (1829), minister's house and period cottages.

Church of St Mary, page 97.

In the locality: Felbrigg Lakeside and Woodland Walks, page 57; Barton Broad, page 64; Hickling Broad National Nature Reserve, page 66; How Hill, pages 67 and 121; churches at Happisburgh, page 87; North Walsham, page 88; and Tunstead, page 95; Alby Gardens, page 98; Beeston Hall and Gardens, page 98; Felbrigg Hall, page 100; Hoveton Hall Gardens, page 101; North Walsham to Dilham Canal, page 116; Potter Heigham Medieval Bridge, page 117; Sutton Windmill, page 123; Alby Craft Centre, page 125; Wroxham Barns, page 129. See also North Walsham, page 32; Wroxham, below.

Wroxham
Early closing Wednesday, except in summer.
This large village is known as the capital of the Broads and it is a prime centre for hiring sailing craft and launches and for day cruises. Strictly, the area north of the river Bure is Hoveton and it is here that the shopping and tourist centre has developed, with more than twenty boatyards, yacht and chandlery stores, as well as Roys, said to be the 'world's largest village store'. A narrow humpbacked bridge over the Bure links Hoveton with Wroxham proper, a more exclusive residential area with boathouses and private staithes on the river. The fifteenth-century church of St Mary once stood at the centre of the village and there are some interesting old buildings nearby.

Hoveton Great Broad Nature Trail, page

67; **Wroxham Broad**, page 73; **Hoveton Hall Gardens**, page 101; **Wroxham Barns**, page 129.

In the locality: Barton Broad, page 64; Belaugh, page 64; Cockshoot Broad, page 64; How Hill, pages 67 and 121; Ranworth Broad and Conservation Centre, page 70; St Benet's Abbey, page 81; churches at Ludham, page 88; Ranworth, page 91; South Burlingham, page 94; Tunstead, page 95; and Worstead, page 97; Beeston Hall and Gardens, page 98; Fairhaven Garden Trust, page 99; Bure Valley Railway, page 115; St Benet's Abbey Mill, page 122; Redwings Horse Sanctuary, page 129.

Wymondham
Early closing Wednesday; market day Friday.

Wymondham (pronounced 'Windam') has more listed buildings than any similar-sized town in the county, most of them built after the disastrous fire in 1615. The streets radiate from the market place, where there is an octagonal market building (1618) of timber, one of only three such buildings remaining in England. One early building which survived the fire is the fifteenth-century Green Dragon in Church Street; it shows signs of charring on some timbers. Wherever you walk in Wymondham, the twin towers of the beautiful abbey dominate the skyline. There is a small museum, which tells the story of the town, which was once an important weaving centre. The Kett brothers (see page 132), who led a rebellion in 1549 against the enclosure of common land, were born in the town. Today Wymondham is growing fast as a commuter town for Norwich.

Wymondham Abbey, page 83; **church of St Mary and St Thomas of Canterbury**, page 97; **Wymondham Heritage Museum**, page 114.

In the locality: Ashwellthorpe Wood, page 56; Arminghall Henge Monument, page 74; Caistor St Edmund Roman Town, page 74; New Buckenham Castle, page 79; churches at Attleborough, page 84; Framingham Earl, page 87; Hingham, page 87; and Shelton, page 94; Industrial Steam Museum, page 105; Wicklewood Windmill, page 124; Banham Zoo, page 125.

3
Coast and countryside

Nature reserves and other countryside sites in the Broads are described in chapter 4.

Ashwellthorpe Wood (OS 144: TM 140980). 2¹/2 miles (4 km) south-east of Wymondham. Norfolk Naturalists Trust. Telephone: 0603 625540.
Open all year.

This ancient woodland, dating back to Domesday, includes hornbeam trees which were once coppiced to provide material for the local brush factory. Spectacular spring flowers include bluebells, ramsons, early purple and bird's nest orchids.

Bacton Wood Forest Trail. Information: Forestry Commission, Horsford, Norwich NR10 3AD. Telephone: 0603 898245. 2¹/2 miles (4 km) north-east of North Walsham.
Open daily.

There are three waymarked walks, the longest 3 miles (5 km), starting from the picnic site on the north-east corner of the wood, known locally as Witton Woods. Thirty species of tree grow here and the wood contains evidence of charcoal burning in the middle ages.

Blakeney Point. National Trust. Information: telephone 0263 740480 (summer only) or 032875 401.
Open daily.

The point is a 100 acre (40 hectare) spit of shingle and sand-dune which has built up west of Cley and has been stabilised by vegetation. Terns, oystercatcher and ringed plover are among the nesting birds. Large flocks of geese overwinter and rare migrant birds appear in the spring and autumn. Seals can be seen on the nearby sandspit. There is a path to the point from Cley (3 miles, 5 km) along the shingle bank, or boatmen will row you over from Morston or Blakeney when the tide is right. On the point there are walkways for the less adventurous and disabled, an information centre and light refreshments.

Blickling Park Walks, Blickling Hall, Blickling, Norwich NR11 6NF. Telephone: 0263 733084. National Trust.
Open daily.

To the north of the hall there is a large artificial lake surrounded by fields and woodland and with a footpath round three sides of it. In winter it attracts migrating swans and other waterfowl. There is also a walk to the mausoleum about ³/4 mile (1 km) north of the hall. The park is open throughout the year.

Brancaster Manor Recreation Area. National Trust. Information: Dial House, Brancaster Staithe, Brancaster PE31 8BW. Telephone: 0485 210719.
Open daily.

The sand-dunes, reclaimed marsh and shore form a large recreational area, parts of which are of interest to naturalists. Access is from Beach Road and a car park is provided. There is a popular beach but bathers should take care at all states of the tide and should not cross the harbour channel at low water. For those who wish to explore further afield, the National Trust operates a cycle hire scheme from Dial House.

Cley Marshes (including Arnold's Marsh). Norfolk Naturalists Trust (and National Trust). Warden: Watchers' Cottage, Cley-next-the-Sea, Holt NR25 7RZ. Telephone: 0263 740380.
Open April to October. Closed Mondays except Bank Holidays. Admission by permit obtainable at the Visitors' Centre.

These saltmarshes overlooking the North Sea became the first nature reserve in England in 1926, with the object of establishing a breeding sanctuary for birds and to induce lost species to return. Today avocet, ruff, bearded tit, bittern and garganey are regularly seen. The reserve is probably the best site for seeing rare birds in mainland Britain. To encourage migrants, scrapes have been excavated to form shallow pools. Access to the hides is via walkways but the public footpath along the east bank also provides good views. There is an information centre and a car park on the landward side of the A149 between Cley and Salthouse.

East Winch Common (OS 132: TF 698160). Near King's Lynn off the A47.
Open all year.
East Winch Common is one of the few large remnants of the heathland that once covered the sandy soils of west Norfolk. It is covered with heather and moor grass but there are also marshy areas and pools. Plants include dodder, sundew and marsh gentian. Several pairs of nightingale breed here, as well as blackcap, chiffchaff and other warblers. The pools provide a habitat for dragonflies and damselflies.

East Wretham Heath (OS 144: TL 913887). 4 miles (6 km) north of Thetford on A1075. Norfolk Naturalists Trust. Telephone: 0603 625540.
Open daily.
This is true Breckland heath, unchanged by afforestation, where plants and animals not often seen in England can be found. The nature trail includes typical Breckland features such as meres, groups of pines, marlpits, wild flowers of the heath, deer, red squirrel and birds such as crossbill and goldcrest.

Felbrigg Lakeside and Woodland Walks, Felbrigg Hall, Cromer NR11 8PR. Telephone: 0263 837444.
Open daily.
These are gentle walks in the park surrounding the hall, one through ancient coppiced woods and plantations made in the seventeenth and eighteenth centuries, and another across the park to the lake. Dogs are not allowed on the lakeside walk.

Foxley Wood Nature Reserve (OS 133: TG 049229). Between North Elmham and Reepham on the B1145. Norfolk Naturalists Trust. Telephone: 0603 625540.

Open daily except Thursdays.
This is the largest ancient woodland in Norfolk and dates back to Domesday Book. There is a rich variety of tree species and in the spring there is a profusion of wild flowers, in summer a variety of butterflies and in autumn fungi. Three species of woodpecker can be heard all round the year.

Hoe Rough, near Gressenhall (OS 132: TF 978168). Norfolk Naturalists Trust. Telephone: 0603 625540.
Open all year.
This is an area of unimproved grassland interspersed with woodland, mossy heath, ponds and spectacular anthills. The huge oak at the entrance is said to be 330 years old.

Holkham Lake Walk and Farm Walk, Holkham Hall, Wells-next-the-Sea NR23 1AB. Information: telephone 0328 710227.
Open daily.
There are two circular walks, each of about 3 miles (5 km), through a beautiful deer park on the Holkham estate. The Lake Walk starts at the North Gates car park and passes the church and the monument to Coke of Norfolk. The large artificial lake has populations of Canada and Egyptian geese and in winter it is visited by greylag geese and other migrant waterfowl. The Farm Walk starts at the South Lodge car park and runs through farmland transformed by Coke's agricultural reforms and passes the Obelisk and Great Barn.

Holkham National Nature Reserve. English Nature and Holkham Estate. NCC warden: Holkham Estate Office, Holkham, Wells-next-the-Sea NR23 1AB. Telephone: 0328 711183 (permits: 0328 710277).
Open daily.
This is the largest National Nature Reserve in England, extending over 10,000 acres (nearly 4000 hectares) of marshes, dunes and intertidal mudflats along 9 miles (14 km) of coast from Burnham Overy to Blakeney. It is an area rich in bird life and includes a noisy communal nesting site for terns. Other breeding birds include oystercatcher, shelduck, redshank, ringed plover, mallard, reed bunting

and kingfisher. In winter it is a refuge for snow bunting, knot, turnstone, golden plover and other migrants. The dunes between Holkham and Wells have been planted with pines, the seeds of which attract red squirrels and goldcrest. Freshwater pools further inland provide habitats for natterjack toads and frogs. Access to the reserve is unrestricted but visitors are asked to keep to the paths. The western part is accessible on foot along the sea wall from Overy Staithe and from the beach at Wells, or by car through Holkham Gap. There is also a footpath along the southern edge of the eastern part of the reserve.

Holt Lowes Country Park. Information: Planning Department, North Norfolk District Council, Cromer NR27 9EL. Telephone: 0263 513811. 1 mile (1.6 km) south of Holt on B1149.
Open daily.
These conifer woods and heath cover over 200 acres (80 hectares) on the site of a former racecourse. There are walks and nature trails (including one for disabled people), information boards and an adventure playground.

Honeypot Wood Nature Reserve, near Wendling (OS 132: TF 934143). Norfolk Naturalists Trust. Telephone: 0603 625540.
Open daily.
Spring is a particularly rewarding time to visit this remnant of the wildwood which once covered Norfolk. The woods are being managed in the traditional way by coppicing and there are many wild flowers of the woodland floor to be seen. The reserve is open all the year.

Horsey. 10 miles (16 km) north of Great Yarmouth. (See also Horsey Mere, page 66.)
Open daily.
Here the visitor will be aware of the bleakness and desolation of this exposed coastline, once left to marshmen and wildfowlers and subject to disastrous storms and floods, as in 1953. But this wilderness makes an attractive place for walks and picnics on the beach and dunes in the summer. Swimming from the beach is not recommended.

Kelling Heath Nature Trail. Information: Kelling Heath Caravan Park, Weybourne, Holt NR25 7HW. Telephone: 026370 224.
Open daily.
The heath is of interest to both historians and naturalists and offers fine views over the coast and countryside. There is a 2½ mile (4 km) woodland nature trail, and there are also archaeological remains of stone age and iron age occupation.

Mannington Walks, Mannington Hall, Saxthorpe, Norwich NR11 7BB. Telephone: 026387 4175.
Open daily.
Here there are 20 miles (32 km) of waymarked walks through woods and parkland (see also page 101).

Marriott's Way. Norfolk County Council. Information: Planning Department, County Hall, Martineau Lane, Norwich NR1 2DH. Telephone: 0603 222718, extension 5247.
Open daily.
This is a 7 mile (11 km) route through the countryside for walkers and horse riders, starting at Hellesdon old watermill and following the old Midland and Great Northern Railway line. The walk passes through farmland, woodland and water meadows alongside the river Wensum. The pretty villages of Alderford and Swannington are on the route, and at Attlebridge there is a picnic area. Marriott was the engineer of the railway, which linked Norwich and King's Lynn.

Morston and Stiffkey Marshes. National Trust. Warden: Dial House, Brancaster Staithe, Brancaster PE31 8BW. Telephone: 0485 210719.
Open daily.
These adjoining saltmarshes attract both breeding and migrating birds and have interesting saltmarsh plants such as sea aster and sea lavender, the latter forming carpets of purple flowers in July. The Morston Marshes are dissected by creeks which attract large populations of redshank, shelduck and brent geese in winter. The old undisturbed marshes at Stiffkey stretch over 490 acres (196 ha) and are winter feeding grounds for brent geese,

wigeon and teal. In spring terns breed on the shingle banks. The sand flats are renowned for their cockles, known as 'Stewkey blues'. Morston Marshes are reached along footpaths from Blakeney or Stiffkey or along a cart track from Morston Quay, and access to Stiffkey Marshes is down a cart track called Greenway west of the village.

Narborough Railway Line (OS 132: TF 750118). ¹/₂ mile (1 km) south of Narborough on the unclassified road to Fincham. Norfolk Naturalists Trust. Telephone: 0603 625540. *Open all year.*
This small 6 hectare (15 acre) reserve is part of a disused railway embankment and is notable for the variety of wildflowers and butterflies found here. Altogether 150 species of flower and 26 species of butterfly have been recorded.

Norfolk Coastal Path. Norfolk County Council. Telephone: 0603 222718.
Footpaths and tracks take you across the wild saltmarshes and their tidal creeks and mudflats, along sandy beaches and shingle banks and beside grazing marshes. This is part of the Heritage Coast. The path starts at Hunstanton and continues along the north coast of Norfolk to Sheringham and Cromer, linking with Peddars Way, Weavers Way and Angles Way. Leaflets are available giving details of the walks.

North Denes Beach Little Tern Colony, Great Yarmouth (OS 134: TG 533097). Royal Society for the Protection of Birds. Warden on site during the breeding season (mid May to August). Information: RSPB Norwich, telephone 0603 661662.
About 140 pairs of little tern, England's rarest nesting bird, make use of this nesting site, over three hundred young fledging each year. An area of the beach 200 feet (60 metres) wide is fenced off when the birds return from wintering in Africa in order to protect the nests from intruders, but there are excellent viewing facilities for visitors.

Oxburgh Woodland Walk, Oxburgh Hall, Oxborough, King's Lynn PE33 9PS. Tele-

Little tern and chick at the North Denes Beach RSPB reserve at Great Yarmouth.

phone: 036621 258.
Open at same times as Oxburgh Hall, see page 102.
There is an attractive short woodland walk starting at the hall.

Peddars Way. Information: Planning Department, County Hall, Martineau Lane, Norwich NR1 2DH. Telephone: 0603 222718.
This long-distance path from Knettishall in Suffolk to the north Norfolk coast was opened by the Prince of Wales in 1986. It follows the ancient Peddars Way track (see page 75) through Breckland to the coast at Holme, where it links with the Norfolk Coastal Path (see above) along the coast to Cromer, a total of 65 miles (105 km). The route is full of interest to the naturalist and historian and also offers good distant views over the coast and countryside. There is also a route for horse riders.

Poppyland
This is the name given to the north Norfolk

coast between Cromer and Sidestrand. This area became popular at the beginning of the twentieth century as a place of wild beauty on the edge of the crúmbling cliffs, ablaze with drifts of poppies in midsummer. It inspired many writers, including the poet Swinburne. There are fewer poppies now but the clifftop walk from Cromer lighthouse to Overstrand, part of which goes through a golf course, offers magnificent views. Walkers should avoid the cliff edge. Agate, cornelian, jet and amber may be found on the beaches below and inland there are walks along narrow lanes to Northrepps and Southrepps, or along the beach to Sidestrand.

Ringstead Downs, near Hunstanton (OS 132: TF 705400). National Nature Reserve. Information: telephone 048525 240.
Open all year.
The Downs are an area of 26 acres (10 hectares) of chalk grassland, one of the few such areas in Norfolk. Here are chalkland plants such as rock-rose, stemless thistle, salad burnet, squinancy-wort and wild thyme. Geologically the area is a dry valley cut through chalk by glacial meltwaters. It is a lovely place for walks and picnics and the public footpath runs through it from Hunstanton to Ringstead.

Roman Camp and Beeston Regis Heath, West Runton. National Trust. Information: Blickling Hall, Norwich NR11 6NF. Telephone: 0263 733084.
The National Trust owns about 70 acres (28 hectares) of heathland and woodland known as Roman Camp, the name having no foundation in history. The area includes the highest point in the county, Beacon Hill (340 feet, 112 metres), and remains of iron workings from Saxo-Norman and early medieval times. Woodland birds, the rare red squirrel and, in open areas, adders can be seen. Adders are venomous but usually retreat when people approach. Parts of the adjoining Beeston Regis Heath are also owned by the Trust and from here there are fine views over the coast. There is car parking for both areas at West Runton.

Roydon Common (OS 132: TF 685225). Norfolk Naturalists Trust. 3 miles (5 km)

from King's Lynn on A148, turn off to Roydon and watch for signs to the car park. *Open all year.*
The interesting wetland plants found here make this a good hunting ground for botanists and there are also a variety of species of butterflies and dragonflies. There is a walk through the reserve, starting at the car park.

Salthouse Marsh Nature Reserve, Gramborough Hill and Walsey Hills Watchpoint, Salthouse. Norfolk Naturalists Trust, National Trust and Norfolk Ornithological Association. Information: NNT, telephone 0603 625540; NOA, Walsey Hills Centre, Old ROC Building, Salthouse; telephone: 0263 740094.
Open all year.
The marshes, shingle banks and salt lagoons attract migratory waders in winter and the observation points at Gramborough Hill

Salthouse Marsh.

and Walsey Hills collect and record information on bird arrivals and departures. Permits for the marshes and Gramborough Hill are obtained from the NNT centre at Cley. There is a warden on duty at the NOA information centre at Walsey Hills, on the landward side of the A149 between Salthouse and Cley, and visitors are welcome.

Sandringham Country Park. Information: Park Ranger, Estate Office, Sandringham, King's Lynn PE35 6EN. Telephone: 0553 2675.

There are nature trails through the 741 acres (296 hectares) of woods and heathland on the royal estate, which includes the Dersingham picnic area, south of Dersingham village on the A149.

Scolt Head Island National Nature Reserve. National Trust and Norfolk Naturalists Trust, leased to English Nature. Information: Dial House, Brancaster Staithe, Brancaster PE31 8BW. Telephone: 0485 210719. Warden: 18 Anchorage View, Brancaster PE31 8XD. Telephone: 0485 210330.
Open all year.

This island off the coast north of Brancaster Staithe consists of coastal flats, saltings and dunes and is noted for its nesting colony of Sandwich terns. Large numbers of migratory birds can also be seen here in winter. Access is by boat, two to three hours before and after high tide from Brancaster Staithe by arrangement with local boatmen. There is a nature trail from the landing point, over the dunes and along the beach. The reserve is open throughout the year.

Snettisham Nature Reserve. Royal Society for the Protection of Birds. Warden: 13 Beach Road, Snettisham PE31 6HD. Information: telephone RSPB, 0603 661662. 3 miles (5 km) west of Dersingham.
Open all year.

The reserve comprises over 3000 acres (1200 hectares) of intertidal sand and mudflats and includes abandoned gravel pits. The area attracts large numbers of birds in winter, including pink-footed goose, ringed plover, oystercatcher, shelduck and tern. The roost of

thousands of wading birds at high tide can be spectacular. Ringed plover, tern, oystercatcher and shelduck are among the birds that breed here. Access is along a shingle bank. Cars must be left at Snettisham Beach car park.

Sparham Pools (OS 144: TF 073178). Near Lyng off the A1067 Norwich to Fakenham road. Norfolk Naturalists Trust. Telephone: 0603 625540.
Open all year.

These wartime gravel workings have mellowed into a nature reserve with pools intermixed with oak woodland, heather and gorse scrub and moss-covered patches offering habitats for a wide variety of plant and animal life. Woodpecker, waterfowl, tern, heron, sand martin and crested grebe may all be seen here, as may dragonflies. The reserve is particularly rich in wild flowers in the spring.

Thetford Forest Walks. Information: Forestry Commission, Santon Downham, Suffolk IP27 0TJ. Telephone: 0842 810271.

The planting of 80 square miles (207 sq km) of mainly coniferous forests in Breckland has been criticised by environmentalists because of the loss of a wild area and the uniformity the forests impose on the heath. However, now that the forests are mature (and productive) they have a certain grandeur and their own wildlife. They are strongholds for red as well as grey squirrel, deer and more than seventy different breeding birds. Even the stone curlew, so typical of Breckland, is returning, and the planting of broad-leaved trees has added variety.

There are a number of waymarked walks and picnic places: for example, there is a picnic site at Great Hockham just off the A1075, and the Thetford Bird Trail, an attractive walk of 3 1/2 miles (5 km) through forests and along the banks of the Little Ouse, starts at Santon Downham. Details are available from the Forestry Commission. Some parts of the forest are within the Ministry of Defence battle area and not accessible to the public.

Thetford High Lodge Forest Centre. Signposted off B1107 near Brandon. Forestry Commission, Santon Downham, Brandon

IP27 0TJ. Telephone: 0842 810271.
Open daily from Easter to the end of September.

The Forest Centre is a new development near the site of an iron age settlement, where Roman pottery has also been found. In the 1930s this was a labour camp and after the Second World War it was used as a home for Polish workers. More recently it has been used for filming *Dad's Army* and as a Forestry Commission office. The Centre has a play area, a wayfaring course, a squirrel scamper and tea rooms. Cycles are available for hire and there is a hide for viewing deer and birds.

Thompson Common (OS 144: TL 934967). Norfolk Naturalists' Trust. Telephone: 0603 625540. 5 miles (8 km) south of Watton on A1075.
Open all year.

This attractive reserve in Breckland consists of grassland, scrub and woodland with pingos (shallow ponds formed during the ice age). The reserve is particularly rich in marsh and woodland plants, and the water violets in the pingos from mid to late May are outstanding. There are two waymarked nature trails open at all times – a short one starting at Butters' Hall Lane car park and a longer one starting at the main car park at Thompson Water. Shetland ponies and roe deer graze the common and the alder trees are cut back to maintain the open areas of grassland.

Thursford Wood (OS 132: TF 979333). 1 mile (1.6 km) west of Thursford. Norfolk Naturalists Trust. Telephone: 0603 625540.
Open daily.

This medieval wood pasture contains some of the oldest trees in the county. There are distinctive gnarled oaks and a great variety of shrubs and trees planted by the previous owners (who are buried in a small plot in the centre of the wood.)

Titchwell Marsh Nature Reserve, near Thornham. Royal Society for the Protection of Birds. Warden: Three Horseshoes Cottage, Titchwell PE31 8BB. Telephone: 0485 210432.

This marsh was reclaimed for agricultural use in the eighteenth century but the 1953 floods destroyed much of the defensive wall and the fields reverted to saltmarsh. A wide variety of birds breed here, including shelduck, reed bunting, redshank and pipits on the saltmarsh, marsh harrier and bittern in the reedbeds, avocet on the brackish marsh, and whitethroat and warblers in the scrub. Winter visitors include ruff, snipe, twite and brent goose. The reserve is open throughout the year, the information centre in the summer only. Hides are provided. There is a car park adjacent with access from the A149 between Thornham and Titchwell.

Wash Coastal Path. Norfolk and Lincolnshire County Councils.
Open all year.

This 10 mile (16 km) walk skirts the undeveloped coastal area of the Wash and follows the top of the outer sea defence bank between West Lynn in Norfolk and East Bank Picnic Place near Sutton Bridge in Lincolnshire. To the north are wild saltmarshes and tidal flats rich in wildlife and there are distant views of stretches of the Norfolk and Lincolnshire coasts. The West Lynn starting point (OS 132: TF 613203) is near the ferry along a rough track to the sea bank. Please note that tidal marshes can be dangerous and walkers should keep to the sea banks.

Wayland Wood, near Watton (OS 144: TL 925996). Norfolk Naturalists Trust. Information: NNT, telephone 0603 625540. 1 mile (1.6 km) south of Watton on A1075.
Open all year.

This is one of the few areas of medieval woodland to survive in Norfolk. According to local legend it was the setting for the story of the Babes in the Wood. The wood is managed in the traditional way by the NNT as coppice with standards. The underwood consists of bird cherry with hazel and the flora is particularly attractive in spring and early summer. The reserve is open at all times.

Weavers' Way. Norfolk County Council.

This is a 15 mile (24 km) waymarked recreational route for walkers and cyclists between Blickling and Stalham, with extensions from Blickling to Cromer (14 miles, 22 km) and from Stalham to Great Yarmouth through Broadland (see page 71). The walk takes its name from the important weaving industry which flourished in the area between the twelfth and eighteenth centuries.

Weeting Heath. Norfolk Naturalists Trust and English Nature. Telephone: 0842 827615; (winter) 0603 625540.
Open April to August. Bird hides open only in the summer.

This is a good example of Breckland chalk grassland on which rabbits formerly flourished. Myxomatosis in the mid 1950s caused a sharp decline in the numbers of rabbits but they are now increasing again and the typical vegetation is returning. Stone curlew and wheatear are here in good numbers and maiden pink and spiked speedwell may be seen. Permits to use bird hides are obtainable from the warden.

Welney Wildfowl Refuge. The Wildfowl Trust, Pintail House, Hundred Foot Bank, Welney, Wisbech, Cambridgeshire PE14 9TN. Telephone: 0353 860711.
Open daily except at Christmas and from November to February for winter evening visits. Pre-booking essential.

The refuge is situated on the east end of the Ouse Washes, one of Europe's most important wintering grounds for wildfowl. The numbers feeding there in winter are spectacular. Swans, widgeon, pochard and pintail duck are there in thousands. Floodlighting at night enables visitors to see the birds roosting around the lagoon. When the waters recede in the spring, the refuge provides safe nesting sites for such birds as black tern, ruff and black-tailed godwit. There are hides, an excellent observatory, information displays and a nature trail (summer only).

West Runton Cliffs and Beach
Here glacial cliffs meet the sea and many animal fossils have been found, including bones of elephants and hippopotamuses. On the beach the chalk which underlies Norfolk comes to the surface and the rocky shore provides habitats for a variety of shore life. It is important not to disturb the rocks.

Winterton Dunes National Nature Reserve, Winterton-on-Sea. Information: English Nature, 60 Braconaale, Norwich NR1 2BE. Telephone: 0603 620558.

This is an acid dune area, rare in East Anglia, which has uncommon plants such as cross-leaved heath and royal fern. The rare natterjack toad is also found here. There is an important breeding colony of terns on part of the dunes, and other breeding birds include whitethroat, chiffchaff and other species of warbler. Winter visitors include brambling, redpoll, siskin and redwing. Adders are found here, so special care is needed, although they are shy creatures and there is little risk. There is a warden on the site during the nesting season.

Wiveton Downs Picnic Area. Norfolk County Council. Information: Planning Department, County Hall, Martineau Lane, Norwich NR1 2DH. Telephone: 0603 222718. 1 mile (1.6 km) south of Blakeney.

This is a quiet wild place for informal picnics with good views over the countryside and the sea, and there are many wild flowers. Adders are present, so care should be taken.

Yare Valley Walk. City of Norwich Amenities, 15 Chapel Field East, Norwich NR2 1RN. Telephone: 0603 622233.

This walk along the banks of the river Yare and through the university campus to the villages of Cringleford, Eaton and Keswick starts at the car park at Earlham Hall. It is best taken in two sections, the first through to the university's artificial broad and back, a pleasantly rural walk. For the second section, start at the Marston Lane car park off the Ipswich road and walk through Eaton Marshes to the village and then down Church Lane to Eaton Common and Keswick Mill.

4

The Broads

Barton Broad. Norfolk Naturalists' Trust. *Open all year.*

Above Irstead Shoals the river Ant spreads out to form one of the most picturesque broads. This is a good place for sailing, rowing and fishing and there are pleasant walks around Barton Turf, a nearby village which originated as a centre for cutting turf or peat. From Barton church there is a walk to the staithe and on to the village of Neatishead.

Belaugh. Between Wroxham and Coltishall on the river Bure.

Belaugh (pronounced 'Beela') was a favourite place of Sir John Betjeman. There is a small staithe and boatyard, good fishing and a fine church. The broad, which is privately owned, was given a new lease of life by the Broads Authority in 1987 when thousands of gallons of sludge and debris were pumped out.

Berney Marshes (OS 134: TG 460050). Royal Society for the Protection of Birds. Warden: Ashtree Farm, Breydon Marine, Burgh Castle, Great Yarmouth NR31 9PZ. Information: RSPB (Norwich). Telephone: 0603 661662. *Open all year.*

The marshes are reached by boat or by train (Berney Arms station) or along signposted paths from Halvergate, a distance of 2 miles (3 km). The best views are from footpaths along the riverbanks or from Burgh Castle or Berney Arms windmill (see page 118). This marshland area was traditionally flooded for much of the winter and early spring, forming a unique landscape and a feeding ground for waders and wildfowl. More efficient drainage in recent years for agricultural purposes dried out much of the wetland but the RSPB is returning the marshes to the traditional form of management and so is restoring them as a feeding and breeding ground for birds.

Bramerton Woods End
Open all year.

This is one of the many places on the Yare which once had a ferry (hence the Ferry Boat Inn). It has long been a favourite picnic place for people from Norwich, which is only 4 miles (6 km) away.

Breydon Water Local Nature Reserve (OS 134: TG 495070). *Open all year.*

This large expanse of water just west of Great Yarmouth provides exciting sailing, especially in a fresh wind. It is a remnant of the huge estuary which once extended as far as Beccles and Norwich. Throughout the year there are large numbers of birds at Breydon, among them shelduck, cormorant and mute swan, and massive gull roosts. Goldeneye and other diving ducks are seen in winter and at low tide oystercatcher, dunlin, redshank and curlew feed on the exposed mud. Marshland flowers, butterflies and dragonflies are also here in profusion. Footpaths from Great Yarmouth and Burgh Castle offer good views over the tidal waters and mudflats.

Cockshoot Broad (OS 134: TG 345164). Norfolk Naturalists Trust and English Nature. The Broad can be reached by car along Ferry Road from Woodbastwick. *Open all year.*

A signposted nature trail leads from the car park opposite the Ferry Boat Inn to a bird observation hide overlooking the broad. The Broads Authority has sealed off the broad from the river Bure and removed mud and debris, with dramatic results. The water is now clear and many lost species of plants and other wildlife are returning.

Filby Broad. West of the village of Filby on A1064. *Open all year.*

Filby, Ormesby and Rollesby Broads,

Hickling Broad.

Toad Hole Cottage at How Hill.

known as the Trinity Broads, were originally one but are now a chain of lakes with no navigable links with the river Bure. Filby, like most of the Broads, was formed when peat diggings, worked in Saxon and early medieval times, later became flooded. Filby is a beautiful stretch of water with reeds and yellow iris along its banks. There are landing stages for local boats, a picnic site, walkways and a bird observation hide.

Fritton Decoy and Lake. Off B1074 between St Olaves and Great Yarmouth.
Open during summer months from April.

The lake is accessible to the public through the Fritton Lake Country Park (telephone 0493 488208 for information), which offers boating, pony rides, beautiful gardens, craft workshops and an adventure playground. There is also a windsurfing school (telephone 0493 488378). The lake is surrounded by woodland and is most attractive. The decoy was used to catch wild ducks by feeding them with corn and then luring them into nets with the help of specially trained tame ducks.

Haddiscoe Marshes. Alongside the river Waveney, 12 miles (19 km) down river from Beccles.
Open all year.

This is a good place for birdwatching and for long walks over the marshes through typical Broadland countryside. Start at St Olaves, where there is a car park, or from Haddiscoe Bridge, where there are moorings for boats, or from Haddiscoe railway station.

Hardley Flood. Norfolk Naturalists Trust. Telephone: 0603 625540.
Open all year.

This nature reserve covers 90 acres (36 ha) and is part of an area of marshland alongside the river Chet north-east of Loddon. There are good footpaths from Chedgrave church to the Flood, where migrant birds such as teal, shoveller and shelduck gather in winter, and oystercatcher and terns in the spring. Breeding birds include the common tern. Hides are available.

Hardley Cross nearby marks the boundary between the Norwich and Yarmouth navigation authorities. It was once the site of annual celebrations between the two communities.

Hickling Broad National Nature Reserve. Norfolk Naturalists Trust. Telephone: 0692 598276.
Open daily except Tuesdays. Water trail Tuesdays, Wednesdays and Thursdays in May and September and Mondays to Fridays from June to August.

The reserve consists of reedbeds with open water and is one of the best areas in which to observe the plants and wildlife of the Broads. Swallowtail butterfly, marsh harrier and bearded tit are among the many interesting species seen here. There are two walking trails starting from the NNT car park in Stubb Road, and permits can be purchased from the information hut, also in Stubb Road. On most days in the summer there is also a water trail starting from the staithe near the Pleasure Boat Inn. The NNT warden takes visitors by boat to bird hides, reedbeds and an observation tower, 60 feet (18 metres) high, in woodland. Advance booking through the warden is essential. The water trail affords excellent views of the broad, which was once an estuary but was later extended by peat and clay digging in the middle ages.

Horsey Mere (OS 134: TG 450220). National Trust. Information: National Trust, Blickling NR11 6NF. Telephone: 0263 733471.
Open during summer months.

The mere is part of a Site of Special Scientific Interest on 2000 acres (800 hectares) of marshland, marrams and farmland. It is part of the Broads but has brackish water as a result of seepage from the sea. Many rare birds are seen here, including the marsh harrier, osprey, black tern, gadwall and bittern. Horsey Windpump (see page 121) stands alongside the dyke leading to the mere, where there is a private staithe. Pleasure boats can tie up here and the staithe is also used by boats transporting the reed and sedge harvest. Horsey Mere is linked by dykes to Heigham Sound and the river Thurne.

Loading reeds at Horsey Mill.

Hoveton Great Broad Nature Trail and Bure Marshes. English Nature.
Open Monday to Friday, May to mid September.
   A mile (1.6 km) downstream from Wroxham Broad on the left bank of the channel there is a mooring place on an island in the middle of Hoveton Great Broad. The island is largely covered with carr woodland and has an interesting nature trail, which is accessible only by boat.

How Hill, Ludham, Great Yarmouth NR29 5PG. Telephone: 069262 763. How Hill Trust and the Broads Authority.
Open daily June to September and at Easter, half terms and Saturdays and Sundays in October.
   How Hill was formerly a private estate but now it is a centre for field studies and conferences. The thatched house, built in 1904, is an environmental centre and Toad Hole Cottage, once a marshman's home, is a museum de-

voted to the marshmen. There is a nature trail through typical Broadland habitats and a wildlife water trail by electric launch. The staithe below the house is used by pleasure boats and boats collecting the reed and sedge harvest. The garden at How Hill is open on advertised days in early summer when the azaleas are in flower.

Langley Dyke and Staithe (OS 134: TG 369030).
Open all year.
   This dyke, which is navigable to small boats, leads from the river Yare to the small village of Langley, where there was once a magnificent abbey. The Wherry Inn on the road leading to the staithe had its origins in the days when these waterways were busy with wherries. There is an interesting walk (4 miles, 6 km) by the river from the Wherry Inn around Langley Marsh to Langley Street and back to the inn, making a detour towards Langley Green to see the remains of the abbey.

Malthouse Broad from the tower of Ranworth church.

The Norfolk Naturalists Trust Conservation Centre at Ranworth.

Greyfriars' Tower, King's Lynn.

Martham Broad Nature Reserve. Norfolk
Naturalists Trust. Information: NNT, telephone 0603 625540.
Open all year.
This broad on the river Thurne to the north
of the village of Martham is one of the most
attractive in Broadland. Much of it is too
shallow for boats although there is a navigable channel through it. The broad has a rich
diversity of Broadland plants and the wildlife
includes bittern, bearded tit and the swallowtail butterfly. The reserve extends over 101
acres (40 ha) and is a Site of Special Scientific Interest. Access is along a footpath from
the village.

Ormesby Broad
This is the most northerly of the Trinity
Broads (see Filby Broad, page 64) and it is
crossed by the Great Yarmouth to Stalham
road (A149) at its southern end. Like Filby, it
is relatively unpolluted and most attractive.
Boats are available for hire and the fishing is
excellent. One can walk from the broad to the
village along minor roads in order to see the
church.

Ranworth Broad and Conservation Centre. Norfolk Naturalists Trust. Conservation
Centre: telephone 0603 270479. 1 mile (1.6
km) west of Ranworth village.
*Open Sundays to Thursdays and Saturday
afternoons April to October; also bank holidays and half terms.*
The inner broad is closed to navigation but
a nature trail starting from the signboard on
the road below the church leads to Ranworth
Broad and the conservation centre. The route
is waymarked and there are information
boards. The centre is housed in a timber and
thatch building floating on pontoons and
moored between Malthouse Broad and Ranworth Broad. There are displays on the
Broadland environment and the gallery gives
excellent views over the broad and can be
used for birdwatching.

River Bure Walk. Information: Hoveton
tourist information centre, telephone 06053
2281.
Windpumps, wildlife, busy waterways and

the ruins of St Benet's Abbey can be seen on
this 7 mile (11 km) waymarked walk, which
starts from the car park at either Upton or
South Walsham. The route runs alongside the
rivers Bure and Thurne.

Salhouse Broad
This small broad, just south of Wroxham
and Great Hoveton Broad, is hidden among
trees alongside the Bure. There are good
moorings at the staithe and a path to the
village of Salhouse, which takes its name
from the sallows or willows found here in
abundance. The church at Salhouse dates to
the twelfth century.

South Walsham Broad
Fleet Dyke connects this broad with the
river Bure. The broad is in two parts. The
deeper, tidal, eastern end has a public staithe,
a boatyard and houses along the waterside; no
landing, fishing or swimming is allowed. The
western end, which is shallower, is privately
owned. The village of South Walsham is
worth exploring and Upton Fen nature
reserve is only a short walk away.

Strumpshaw Fen Nature Reserve (OS 134:
TG 344065). Royal Society for the Protection
of Birds. Warden: Staithe Cottage, Low Road,
Strumpshaw NR13 4HS. Telephone: RSPB
(Norwich) 0603 661662. 8 miles (13 km) east
of Norwich on A47.
Open all year.
This 700 acre (280 ha) reserve in the Yare
valley consists of two broads and a large fen
with reed and sedge beds, willow and alder
stands. It is an excellent place to see Broadland birds and the signposted wild-flower
walk is spectacularly beautiful in July and
August. There are educational displays and
bird hides at the reserve and it is open throughout the year. The entrance to the reserve is
across the level crossing from the car park,
reached by turning sharp right and right again
into Low Road from Brundall.

Surlingham Church Marsh (OS 143: TG
306064). Royal Society for the Protection of
Birds. Warden: 2 Chapel Cottages, The Green,
Surlingham NR14 7AG. Information: RSPB,

telephone 0603 661662. Park alongside Surlingham church and approach the reserve along a signposted footpath.
Open all year.

The reserve's waterways have been isolated from the polluted waters of the river Yare to allow the pools and dykes to grow a variety of aquatic plants once more and to improve the area as a habitat for the many birds to be seen here – reed and sedge warbler, great crested grebe, Canada goose, kingfisher, tufted duck and teal. Migratory birds seen here include greenshank, dunlin, osprey and grey plover. There is a waymarked walk round the reserve.

Sutton Broad

This broad, now no wider than the river, stretches for about a mile on the eastern bank of the river Ant, just south of Stalham. There is a staithe at the eastern end. The A149 passes between the staithe and the village, where there is a privately owned windmill with a Broads museum (see page 123).

Upton Fen. Norfolk Naturalists Trust. Telephone: 0603 270479.
Open all year.

Many rare marshland plants and dragonflies can be seen here in summer on these unspoilt marshes, which have been used for grazing since Saxon times. There is a 7 mile (11 km) waymarked walk from South Walsham to Upton. Upton Broad, west of the village, is unusual in being fed from springs and so has exceptionally fresh, clear water. It cannot be reached by boat from the Bure but boats can be hired on the broad. There is good fishing and interesting plants and wildlife can be seen. In Upton churchyard there is a headstone with a carving of a wherry.

Weavers' Way: Stalham to Great Yarmouth.

This is a cross-country walk developed by Norfolk County Council, originally from Blickling to Stalham (see page 62) but now extended to Cromer and also through Broadland to Yarmouth. The routes are well signposted and descriptive leaflets are available from tourist information centres. The Broadland section of the walk covers 27 miles (43 km), mostly along public footpaths and tracks, with some short stretches along minor roads. The route goes through Stalham, Sutton and Hickling in the Ant valley, then to Bastwick, Repps and Thurne in the Thurne valley. It next follows the Bure to Acle and passes through Tunstall and Halvergate to the Berney Arms and finally along the river Yare to Great Yarmouth.

Wherries. Information: Norfolk Wherry Trust, 14 Mount Pleasant, Norwich. Telephone: 0603 505815. Wherry yacht charter: P. J. A. Bower, Bowton House, Hartwell Road, The Avenue, Wroxham NR12 8TL. Telephone: 06053 2470.

Before the First World War dozens of black-sailed wherries plied the Broads carrying cargo, as they had done for two hundred years. As road and rail took over from water transport, the wherries went out of service and many were left to rot, for example at Surlingham Broad, where there is a wherry 'graveyard'. But in 1949 the Norfolk Wherry Trust was formed and the wherry *Albion* was brought back into use. Since then others have been restored, and some are now available for charter.

Whitlingham Country Park. Norwich City Council.

This riverside area has long been a leisure area for the people of Norwich, which is only 2 miles (3 km) away. It is easily reached along Whitlingham Lane off the A146 Norwich to Beccles road or by boat along a dyke on the north bank of the Yare. This is a good place for walks and picnics.

Womack Water, off the river Thurne, near Ludham.

This was formerly a small broad but is now little more than a winding channel through a reed swamp. The channel leads to Womack Staithe and is the best place to moor if you wish to visit Ludham (see page 31). The County Sailing Base, Womack Staithe, Ludham NR29 5QG (telephone 069262 263), has been established here. Instruction is given on sailing yachts, priority being given to school parties.

St Edmund's church at Caistor St Edmund Roman town.

The Roman walls of Burgh Castle.

Wroxham Broad
Open all year.

This is a fine sailing lake ³/₄ mile (1.2 km) long and 250 yards (230 metres) wide with a good depth of water, in the very heart of Broadland. Sailing races are held here under the auspices of the Norfolk Broads Yacht club most weekends during the summer. Alongside the Broad there are busy boatyards, and shops for the yacht crews and holiday-makers.

St Nicholas's, Great Yarmouth, is one of the largest parish churches in England.

5
Places of archaeological interest

Norfolk has more than 24,000 recorded archaeological sites, five hundred of them protected by legislation, but there are relatively few sites with interesting visible remains.

Arminghall Henge Monument (OS 134: TG 239060).

This important site of a timber henge monument stands on the outskirts of Arminghall near the river Tas. It can be seen from a footpath which runs from White Horse Lane to the Lakenham to Caistor St Edmund road and which passes the northern edge of the site. All that remains of the henge are two concentric circles 270 feet (80 metres) in diameter with an entrance causeway. The earthworks have been much reduced by ploughing. Pottery excavated on the site suggests a date of 3000 to 2000 BC. The henge was the focus of religious ceremonies, possibly burial rites.

Bichamditch, Beachamwell, near Marham (OS 143: TF 745084).

Two centuries after the end of Roman rule this defensive dyke was built, crossing the main east to west Roman road at right angles. It was originally 5 miles (8 km) long and ran from Narborough to Beachamwell. It was used to defend the people of west Norfolk from invading Anglo-Saxon groups. Fosse Ditch near Weeting and Devil's Ditch near Garboldisham are similar earthworks.

Brancaster Roman Fort (*Branodunum*) (OS 132: TF 782440). National Trust.

The Romans built this coastal fort in the third century AD as a defence against the Anglo-Saxon raiders. It was a base for cavalry units and a haven for part of the Roman fleet. The site can be approached from a coastal footpath at the edge of the saltmarsh but no masonry remains, only earthworks. Stones from the fort can be seen in the chancel of Brancaster church.

Burgh Castle (*Gariannonum*), near Great Yarmouth (OS 134: TG 475046). English Heritage.
Open daily.

This fort (pronounced 'Burra' Castle) overlooking the Waveney valley between Great Yarmouth and Acle is the best-preserved of the Roman monuments in Norfolk. It is one of a series of coastal forts built late in the third century AD to defend the shore against Anglo-Saxon pirates. It originally stood on a saltwater estuary but this was blocked when the sandspit on which Yarmouth is built was formed. Some massive walls and towers remain of the Roman fort, which was occupied by the Irish monk St Fursey as a monastery in the seventh century. Later the Normans converted it into a castle.

Caister-on-Sea Roman Town (OS 134: TG 518125). English Heritage.

These remains of a Roman site, possibly a fortified town, have been revealed by excavation and include part of a defensive wall, a gateway and buildings along a main street. The town was a commercial port from the second to the fifth century AD. It is not to be confused with Caister Castle (page 78).

Caistor St Edmund Roman Town (*Venta Icenorum*) (OS 134: TG 230035). Norfolk Archaeological Trust.

Farming has largely obliterated the extensive remains of a Roman market town which once existed here but St Edmund's church incorporates fragments in its walls. A car park for the site was established in 1993. It

Aerial view of the neolithic flint mines at Grimes Graves.

has information boards. The ramparts can be walked; the circuit takes about an hour. *Venta Icenorum* was built following the revolt of the Iceni under Queen Boudicca (Boadicea). Norwich Castle Museum has a display of artefacts from the site.

Grimes Graves Neolithic Flint Mines, Weeting (OS 144: TL 817897). English Heritage. Custodian: The Lodge, Grimes Graves, Lynford, Thetford IP24 3TW. Telephone: 0842 810656.
Open daily Easter to September.

More than three hundred pits and shafts have been discovered here in Breckland, 4 miles (6 km) north-east of Brandon. The site has been partly levelled over the centuries but one shaft remains open to the public. The mines were worked for their flints, which were used as cutting tools by stone age people more than four thousand years ago. Flint mining was one of the industries that made farming possible. The mines are open from Easter to September and an exhibition on the site

includes red deer antlers used as picks in the mines. Conducted tours of the mine shaft are available.

Peddars Way (OS 132 and OS 144). From Riddlesworth on the Suffolk border to the coast at Holme.

Shortly after the rebellion of the Iceni in East Anglia in AD 60, the Romans built this road to provide a fast route for soldiers travelling between the Wash and the heart of East Anglia. Originally the road was an impressive structure with raised embankments on some sections where it crossed river valleys, and road widths of up to 45 feet (13.5 metres) have been found. It is now chiefly of interest as part of a long-distance footpath (see page 59) but remains of the Roman road can be seen along the way, for example the embankments at Brettenham, where the road crosses the river Thet.

Warham Iron Age Fort, near Wighton (OS 132: TF 943408).

Aerial view of the iron age fort at Warham.

This pre-Roman war camp was constructed between 25 BC and AD 25 during the iron age. It is the best-preserved of the East Anglian iron age forts and consists of double ramparts and a ditch enclosing an almost circular area of about 3½ acres (1.4 ha). Excavations in 1959 revealed trenches with the remains of a timber palisade and Romano-British pottery sherds. The fort is open to the public and can be approached along a trackway.

Binham Priory.

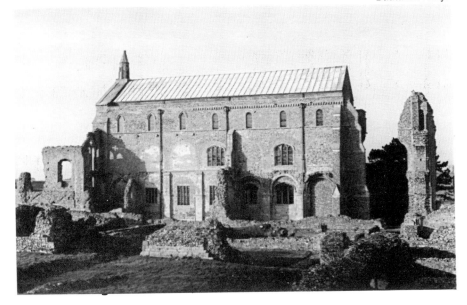

6
Castles and monastic buildings

Norfolk is not a county of castles, chiefly because it was not threatened with invasion after 1200, but it is rich in ruins of religious houses. Norfolk was wealthy in the middle ages and some of that wealth went into the building of monasteries, priories and friaries. No less than seventy once existed in the county. After the Dissolution of the monasteries, the buildings were plundered for building materials and then allowed to fall into decay, but substantial ruins remain.

Baconsthorpe Castle, Baconsthorpe (OS 133: TG 122382). English Heritage.
Open daily.

This moated, semi-fortified house was built by the Heydon family between 1450 and 1486. A ruined gatehouse (of a later date) and remnants of walls and towers are all that remain of the building. In Tudor times the Heydons converted one of the towers into a wool-processing factory, which can still be seen. The family fortunes then declined and in the middle of the seventeenth century much of the 'castle' was demolished and eighteen carts of masonry were sold to Felbrigg Hall (see page 100) for £35. Parts of the ruins were converted into a house by a new owner and alterations and additions continued to be made over the years until it was finally abandoned in 1920. The moat has been excavated and filled with water, a drawbridge leads into a walled enclosure and there is a delightful mere with swans and ducks. The castle is open throughout the year.

Beeston Regis Priory, Beeston Regis Common, near Sheringham (OS 133: TG 168429).
Open daily.

There are extensive remains of the thirteenth-century Augustinian priory near Abbey Farmhouse. The ruins of the 130 foot (40 metre) long church are impressive and there are remains of the cloisters.

Binham Priory, Binham (OS 132: TF 982399). English Heritage.

Open daily.

The priory was founded by the Benedictines in the late eleventh century and continued to grow for four hundred years. After the Dissolution of the monasteries much of the priory was demolished but the beautiful nave, one of the architectural treasures of Norfolk, was kept as the parish church of Our Lady of the Holy Cross. It is a fine example of the Early English style and the west front is particularly admired, even though the thirteenth-century window is bricked up. Inside there are Norman arches, triple sedilia, medieval carved bench ends and a fifteenth-century Seven Sacraments font. In the priory ruins it is still possible to trace the outlines of the cloisters, the refectory, the cellarer's stores, a malting kiln, the brewery, the bakery, the warming room and the guest accommodation. There is a medieval wayside cross on the green adjacent to the priory. Both the priory and the cross are freely accessible to the public.

Broomholm Priory, Bacton (OS 133: TG 351333). On the Walcott side of the village off the B1159 coast road.

The ruins of this Cluniac priory stand in a field within reach of the sea. The priory was founded in 1113 and built in the late Norman and Early English style. The priory became famous in the middle ages as a pilgrimage centre because it owned a relic of the True Cross, a relic mentioned by Chaucer. The ruins are impressive although overgrown. They can be seen by arrangement with the owners of the farmhouse which stands within the ruins.

Burnham Norton Friary, Burnham Norton (OS 132: TF 839428).
Open daily.
This Carmelite friary was founded in 1241; it is now in ruins but the fourteenth-century two-storey gatehouse with flushwork decoration is still impressive. It belongs to the Earl of Leicester but is cared for by the county council.

Caister Castle, West Caister, Great Yarmouth NR30 5SN. Information: telephone the owner, 057284 649.
Open in summer.
Sir John Fastolf built this fortified and moated manor house between 1432 and 1435. It was one of the grandest of the fifteenth-century castles in England and consisted of a great hall, a summer hall, a winter hall, 26 chambers and domestic quarters. After a fire

Castle Acre Priory.

in the sixteenth century the castle fell into disuse, but the ruins are impressive, especially the 98 foot (30 metre) high circular tower. The castle is privately owned and in the grounds there is a very large collection of motor cars and vehicles of all kinds. Steam cars are a speciality.

Castle Acre Bailey Gate, Castle Acre (OS 132: TF 817152). English Heritage.
The only building of the medieval town of Acre to survive more or less intact is this thirteenth-century gateway, which can be seen at the east end of Stock's Green.

Castle Acre Castle, Castle Acre (OS 132: TF 819152). English Heritage.
Open daily.
This has been called 'one of the finest castle earthworks in England' and excavations in the 1970s uncovered the considerable remains of the oblong keep built by the Normans in the eleventh century.

Castle Acre Priory, Castle Acre. Telephone: 0760 755394. English Heritage.
Open daily April to September and Tuesdays to Sundays in winter.
This Cluniac priory in the beautiful Romanesque style was inspired by Cluny Abbey in France and built in the twelfth century. Although there were never more than thirty monks here, relics of saints held by the priory attracted pilgrims from all over Europe. The fine west front of the priory church is still standing but the nave, choir and apse are no more than piles of masonry and flint. In the ruins of the monks' quarters it is possible to identify the place where the wafers for mass were baked, the library, dormitories, latrines, infirmary, kitchen and fishponds. The sixteenth-century prior's lodging and chapel were converted to secular use after the Dissolution of the monasteries and remain more or less intact. There is a small site exhibition.

Castle Rising Castle, Castle Rising, King's Lynn PE31 6AH. Telephone: 0553 631330. English Heritage.
Open daily April to September; Tuesdays to Sundays from October to March; closed 24th

Castle Rising Castle.

to 26th December and 1st January.

The castle dates from 1138 and is a good example of a late Norman motte and bailey. It is set in the centre of massive earthworks covering 12 acres (5 hectares). In 1327 Queen Isabella was imprisoned here and it remained a royal castle until 1544. After being derelict for centuries it has now been restored. A gatehouse leads to the keep, which has walls 8 feet (2.4 metres) thick, and there is an elaborate three-storeyed forebuilding added in the fourteenth century. Inside the keep there is a great hall with staircases leading to bedchambers, a gallery, the chapel and kitchens.

Creake Abbey, North Creake (OS 132: TF 856394). English Heritage.

Open in summer.

The considerable thirteenth-century remains of an abbey founded by the Augustinians in 1206 can be seen here.

Greyfriars' Cloisters, off South Quay, Great Yarmouth (OS 134: TG 525073). English Heritage.

Open daily April to September.

These remains of a thirteenth-century friary include wall paintings and parts of the vault of the only Franciscan cloister to survive in England.

Greyfriars' Tower, King's Lynn. At north end of London Road in a park.

A Franciscan friary was founded in Lynn around 1230 and enlarged in the fourteenth century. All that now remains is the octagonal tower built of brick and stone. It probably owes its survival to the fact that it has served as a landmark for ships entering the port.

Hales Hall. See page 100.

New Buckenham Castle, New Buckenham. Custodian: John Holland, Castle Hill Garage, New Buckenham, Norwich NR16 2AG. Telephone: 0953 860374 (day) or 453998 (evenings).

Open access: keys obtainable from Castle Hill Garage.

In 1151 William the Conqueror's son

William built this castle, one of the earliest circular keeps in England and one of the largest in diameter. The ruins rise to over 45 feet (14 metres) above the level of the moat and the walls are 14 feet (4 metres) thick. The village was built at the same time, on a grid plan.

North Elmham Saxon Cathedral and Bishop's Castle, North Elmham (OS 132: TF 988217). English Heritage.
Open daily.

North Elmham was the seat of a Saxon bishop from AD 631 to 1071, before the bishopric moved first to Thetford and then in 1096 to Norwich. Part of the stone Saxon throne is still preserved in Norwich Cathedral. The stone ruins at the lower level are possibly those of an Anglo-Saxon cathedral but they are more probably the remains of a chapel for an early Norman bishop. The bishops continued to use North Elmham as a country retreat and in the fourteenth century Bishop Dispenser built a fortified house there. He made an earthwork against the walls of the old church, surrounded it with a moat and converted the building into a castellated manor house. The upper part of the ruins we see today is the remains of this building. There

are fine views over the countryside from the ruins.

Norwich Castle, Norwich NR1 3PZ. Telephone: 0603 222222.
Open weekdays and Sunday afternoons.

Soon after the Norman Conquest King William I built a royal castle on an artificial mound in the centre of the Norman settlement in Norwich. The first building was a timber and earth construction but in the twelfth century a keep was built using Caen stone and local carrstone. The original stonework can now be seen only inside the keep. The beautifully decorated Norman doorway can be seen from within the castle. It led to the great hall, chapel and dwelling rooms; below were the store-rooms, and lower still were the dungeons, which were used as a prison from 1220 to 1857. Public executions took place on the castle mound, the last in 1849. Only the prison area was kept in repair and by 1792 the castle was a roofless shell. In the nineteenth century it was converted to a museum (see page 109).

Norwich Cathedral Cloisters, The Close, Norwich. Information: Visitors' Centre, Norwich Cathedral NR1 4DD. Telephone:

The ruins of the 'Anglo-Saxon cathedral' at North Elmham.

The remains of a windmill built into the ruins of St Benet's Abbey at Ludham.

0603 626290.
Open daily.
The wealthiest of all the medieval monasteries in Norfolk was the Benedictine priory attached to the cathedral, founded in 1096. The original Norman buildings were almost completely destroyed in 1272 when the citizens set fire to the monastery. It was later rebuilt. After the Dissolution many of the buildings were again destroyed but the cloisters and fragments of other buildings survived. The carved roof bosses in the cloisters, made between 1297 and 1430, illustrate scenes from the Christian story and secular scenes and are especially fine.

St Andrew's and Blackfriars' Halls, St Andrew's Plain, Norwich NR3 1AU. Telephone: 0603 628477.
Open daily.
The halls were originally the nave and choir of the Blackfriars' convent church in Norwich. Having come to the city in 1226, the Blackfriars, or Dominicans, moved to the present site in 1307, taking over some brick buildings, dating from 1270 to 1307, from

another order. These mostly survive, being now used as the Crypt Coffee Bar and Becket's Chapel. After fire destroyed much of the friars' church in 1413 the present building was erected by Sir Thomas Erpingham but the great east window and six other windows survive from the first church. There is a fine fifteenth-century door.

After the Reformation the city council took over the buildings, and the nave and choir have been used as civic halls since 1542, although in Elizabethan times the choir was used as the church of the city's large Dutch population. The friars' dormitory became a granary, then for a time a nonconformist chapel, and the cloisters were used as a mint, a workhouse and a school. The tower collapsed in 1712. These buildings are the most complete friary complex in Britain and have been in continuous occupation since the thirteenth century.

St Benet's Abbey, Ludham (OS 134: TG 384168).
Open daily.
This important Benedictine abbey was en-

dowed by King Cnut in 1020 and built beside the river Bure among rich grazing marshes in Broadland. It became immensely wealthy but suffered many disasters. It was overwhelmed by floods in 1287, attacked by peasants in 1381 and, when the monasteries were dissolved in the sixteenth century, it was demolished leaving only a few walls and a fourteenth-century gatehouse. In the eighteenth century a windmill (see page 122) was built within the gateway and this has become a favourite subject with artists and photographers. The last abbot was made Bishop of Norwich and the present Bishop holds a service in the ruins on the first Sunday in August. The ruins can be reached by boat or along a footpath from Ludham.

St Faith's Priory, Horsham St Faith, Norwich NR10 3JJ. Telephone: 0603 898093. On A140 Norwich to Cromer road.
Open on advertised days from Easter to September.
This French Benedictine priory was founded in 1105 by Robert Fitzwalter and built from Caen stone from Normandy, like Norwich Cathedral. Upon the Dissolution of the monasteries all but the refectory was destroyed and the contents were dispersed. It became the home of the Southwell family and Robert Southwell, the Jesuit martyr, was born here in 1561. The priory is now a private home. There are superb medieval wall paintings, parts of the Norman cloister, medieval stonework, Tudor panelling and a priest's hole. The priory is open on advertised days from Easter to September, and for groups by arrangement.

St Olaves Priory, St Olaves (OS 134: TM 459996). 5½ miles (9 km) south-west of Great Yarmouth on A143.
Open daily.
The remains of this small Augustinian priory of about 1216 include a small church and part of the cloisters with a brick undercroft, providing a very early example of the use of brick.

Thetford Castle, Thetford (OS 144: TL 873828). East of the town centre.
Open daily.

The castle, now only a mound, was originally the site of an iron age fort. The Norman castle was a timber construction and was demolished in 1173.

Thetford Priory, Thetford (OS 144: TL 866834). English Heritage.
Open daily.
There are extensive remains of this important twelfth-century Cluniac priory on the north side of the A11 overlooking the river Thet. The outlines of a Romanesque-style church and monastic buildings and a fourteenth-century two-storey gateway can be seen. Thetford also has ruins of the church of the Holy Sepulchre (Augustinian) on the

The priory ruins at Walsingham.

Weeting Castle.

B1107 Brandon road (English Heritage) and a Benedictine nunnery on the road to Euston.

Walsingham Abbey, Little Walsingham NR22 6DQ. Telephone: 0328 820259.
Open: April, Wednesdays and Saturdays only; May to September, Wednesdays, Saturdays and Sundays and also on Mondays and Fridays in August.

A large fifteenth-century gateway in the High Street leads into the abbey gardens, to the remains of a twelfth-century Augustinian priory, including the great arch of the east window of the church, the crypt, wells and refectory. The shrine stood to the north of the church and was one of the most visited pilgrim shrines in Europe in the middle ages. The abbey is privately owned and open during the summer, and there are also woodland walks in the grounds.

Weeting Castle, Weeting (OS 144: TL 778891). English Heritage.
Open daily.

This twelfth-century fortified manor house within a rectangular moated enclosure is reputed to have been used by Hereward the Wake as a refuge and features in Charles Kingsley's novel named after him.

Wymondham Abbey, Wymondham.
Open daily.

A Benedictine priory was built here between the twelfth and fifteenth centuries and in 1449 it became an abbey. The cloisters and other monastic buildings have long since disappeared but their location was revealed by aerial photographs in 1979. The abbey church is now the parish church of Wymondham (see page 97).

7
Churches and chapels

Norfolk has more than 650 medieval churches, most of them still in use for worship. Some parishes are not content with one church: Reepham has two and the ruins of a third in the same churchyard! The churches are mainly built of flint, except those in the marshland west of King's Lynn, where stone churches are the rule. Round towers are common and a distinctive feature of the Norfolk countryside. Of nearly 180 still standing in England, 120 are in Norfolk, and there are visible ruins of nine others. They are widely held to be Norman but recent research suggests that they are almost all the work of Saxon craftsmen and that the majority were built before the Norman conquest. There is a particularly interesting cluster of churches with round towers west of Great Yarmouth. Only the finest or most interesting churches are listed below although almost every pre-Reformation Norfolk church has something of interest for the visitor.

Attleborough: Assumption of the Blessed Virgin Mary.

It is surprising to find the Norman tower of this imposing church at the east end of the medieval flint building. The tower stood at the west end of the original Norman church but when a monastery was established here in 1386 a new nave was built west of the tower for use by the laity. At the Dissolution the Norman church was pulled down. The beautiful Decorated windows of the nave of the present church are much admired, as is the fifteenth-century screen, which is one of the most complete in England.

Binham: Our Lady of the Holy Cross.

See Binham Priory, page 77.

Blakeney: St Nicholas.

No one knows why this church has two towers, a substantial western one 104 feet (31 metres) high in the Perpendicular style, and a delicate slender beacon at the east end which may have served as a lighthouse. The chancel is in the Early English style with a beautiful ribbed ceiling but the nave is later (1435), with handsome arcades, clerestory windows and a hammerbeam roof with carved angels. In the churchyard there are good eighteenth-century headstones carved by a local man.

Booton: St Michael and All Angels.

The Reverend Whitwell Elwin, rector of Booton for fifty years until his death in 1900, championed the Gothic revival in church architecture and was wealthy enough to put his ideas into practice by rebuilding the very ordinary church that he found in his parish. The church can be recognised from afar by the forest of pinnacles placed on the twin towers. Elwin built in flint and stone in his version of many Gothic styles and the workmanship is superb.

Brisley: St Bartholomew.

This fine church was built between the late fourteenth century and the fifteenth from wealth created by the wool industry. Last to be built was the magnificent four-stage tower, which has decorative flintwork and niches for statues. Inside, the church is quaintly rustic, with a three-decker Jacobean pulpit, box pews, a minstrels' gallery and carved bench ends, one of which shows a dog carrying off a goose.

The Burnhams. Burnham Deepdale: St Mary. Burnham Market: St Mary. Burnham Norton: St Margaret. Burnham Thorpe: All Saints.

There are seven churches in this cluster of villages (see page 18) but especially note-

Cley church, built when Cley was a prosperous wool port.

worthy is St Mary's at Burnham Deepdale, which has a Saxon round tower and a famous Norman font with a carved frieze showing the labours of the months of the year. The parapet on the tower of St Mary's, Burnham Market, has carved figures and scenes, which are worth viewing through binoculars, and St Margaret's at Burnham Norton has a late Saxon round tower and a painted screen (1548). At Burnham Thorpe there are relics of Nelson in the church where he was baptised.

Castle Acre: St James.
This fifteenth-century church stands on a hilltop overlooking the village and the ruins of the priory and castle (see page 78). Much of the medieval furniture of the church has survived: the high font cover still with its colouring, red gilding, a pulpit with painted panels, parts of a rood screen, bench ends and misericords.

Cawston: St Agnes.
This is one of the great churches in Nor-

folk. In medieval times it was maintained in part by the Plough Guild and today a plough stands in the church. There is also an inscription on the ringers' gallery which begins 'God spede the plow and send us all corn enow for our purpose...'. The tower, started in 1421, is unusual in being faced with stone, probably to strengthen it because an earlier tower had been blown down in 1412. It has an impressive west window and below it a doorway with carvings of a wild man and a dragon. Inside, the hammerbeam roof has carved angels and there are painted figures on the screen.

Cley-next-the-Sea: St Margaret.
When this beautiful church was built in the fourteenth century the river Glaven was busy with sea-going ships and Cley was a wealthy port. Expert stone-masons were employed to build a church in the free-flowing Decorated style with pinnacles, wonderful clerestory windows and battlemented aisles. The Black Death in 1349 and the silting up of the river brought a change of fortunes and the grand design was never realised. The south transept

East Dereham church.

with its beautiful window was blocked off and has been a romantic ruin for three hundred years. In the vast interior there are carvings on the nave arches, carved bench ends and misericords and fine memorial brasses. There is a modern stained glass window in the Lady Chapel showing Cley windmill and local birds. In the churchyard there are interesting eighteenth-century headstones.

Cromer: St Peter and St Paul.

The 160 foot (48 metre) high tower is the tallest in Norfolk and has interesting detail. It has been a valuable landmark for fishermen, many of whose names are recorded on memorials in the church and in the well-kept churchyard. The church is a typical Norfolk flint building of the late fourteenth and fifteenth centuries, much restored in Victorian times and the twentieth century.

East Dereham: St Nicholas.

St Withburga, a local saint of royal blood, established an abbey here in AD 654 which became a place of pilgrimage. A well, said to have sprung from her grave, can be seen beyond the west end of the church and a modern window to the saint has been placed in the

north chapel next to a monument to William Cowper, the poet. The south and north aisles and the Lady Chapel of this imposing church are all of the 1460s. There is a detached belltower (1501) and a squat Decorated crossing tower. There are many interesting details in this church, including a 1468 Seven Sacraments font which is richly carved but defaced.

East Harling: St Peter and St Paul.

The fourteenth-century tower of this church, with its ornate base and decorative parapet, is one of the finest in the county and the whole church, in the Perpendicular style, is virtually unchanged from the time it was built. The Harling (or Herling) family was largely responsible for building it and their bull and unicorn emblems appear in the south aisle roof; there is a family tomb in the Lady Chapel. Among the many splendid things in this church is the fifteenth-century stained glass in the east window. The glass was removed to safety during the Civil War and again in the Second World War. Other treasures include the hammerbeam roof, the clerestory windows, the rood screen and the alabaster tomb (1604) of Sir Thomas Lovell.

Elsing: St Mary the Virgin.

The memorial brass to Sir Hugh Hastings in the chancel of this church, built by Sir Hugh in the fourteenth century, is one of the oldest and most interesting in Britain. The nave of the church is exceptionally wide (40 feet, 12 metres) and there are remnants of fourteenth-century stained glass in the south windows of the chancel, and an elaborate pinnacled font cover of the same date.

Framingham Earl: St Andrew.

The chancel of this tiny church is Anglo-Saxon, with double-splayed circular windows, and excavations in 1984 revealed that it was originally apsed. The tower is also Anglo-Saxon; window mouldings and doorways are Norman. On the outside the flintwork is interesting: huge flints were shaped to provide corner stones for the west end of the nave.

Gooderstone: St George.

A complete set of fifteenth-century benches with pierced backs is one of the glories of this church, built in the fourteenth century in the Decorated style, but still retaining its Norman tower.

Hales: St Margaret.

This very special church has a round tower, a narrow nave with thick walls and an apse at the east end; it was probably built between AD 700 and 800 and is certainly the work of Saxon craftsmen. The Normans added the ornamented north and south doorways and arcaded windows. The interior is colour-washed in cream and there are a plain octagonal font, parts of a medieval screen and a Jacobean pulpit and gallery.

Happisburgh: St Mary.

This flint church looks out over the North Sea towards the treacherous Happisburgh Sands and the tall tower has been a useful landmark for mariners. The church has an impressive octagonal font. In the churchyard there are interesting memorials to sailors lost at sea.

Hingham: St Andrew.

Architects admire this church with its fine high tower and beautiful windows because it is entirely in the Decorated style. The interior was over-restored in the nineteenth century but it is grand and spacious nonetheless. There is a fine memorial to Lord Morley (died 1435), which also once served as an Easter sepulchre. In a niche in the north aisle there is a bust of Abraham Lincoln, whose ancestors came from Hingham.

King's Lynn: St Margaret.

This is a grand church of white Caen stone,

A misericord in St Margaret's church, King's Lynn.

a fitting church for a wealthy community of seafarers and merchants. It was begun in 1104 and has two Norman west towers. The rest of the church was rebuilt in the fourteenth century and the interior was reconstructed again in the eighteenth century following the destruction of the nave, transepts and central lantern in the great storm of 1741. The church has two important brasses, both fourteenth-century.

Little Snoring: St Andrew.

The round flint tower, looking very un-English with its conical top, is probably pre-Conquest and was part of an earlier church. Today's parish church, just a few feet away from the tower, has a Norman doorway, the inner arch of which was reformed in the Early English style. Windows ranging from simple Norman lancets to Tudor have been built into the church. The interior is very simple, the plain furnishings including a Norman font and an eighteenth-century pulpit.

Loddon: Holy Trinity.

Loddon's main square is dominated by this fine Perpendicular church built around 1480. The five-stage tower has two coffin stones at the base, said to commemorate two masons who fell to their deaths during its construction. There is an octagonal font which was defaced in 1642 at a cost, so the churchwardens' accounts reveal, of 6 shillings. The screen has a rare portrayal of St William of Norwich.

Ludham: St Catherine.

This fourteenth-century church stands in the centre of Ludham, its tower dwarfing the houses in the market square. The interior is light and spacious with six-bay aisles. The carvings on the font include one of the abbot of nearby St Benet's Abbey. The screen is one of the finest in Norfolk and has paintings of ten saints and two kings.

North Elmham: St Mary the Virgin.

This impressive church near the ruins of the 'Anglo-Saxon' cathedral (see page 80) is a patchwork of styles from Norman to Tudor, with much subsequent restoration. The screen has fine paintings; it was removed in the

seventeenth century and parts of it were used as flooring for the pews, but it was discovered and reconstructed in the nineteenth century.

North Walsham: St Nicholas.

In spite of its ruined tower, which suffered falls in 1724 and again in 1836, this is a remarkably handsome church. It was built in the fourteenth and fifteenth centuries and the decorative south porch with carvings and pinnacles is noteworthy. Inside there are rood beams with carved bosses, a fifteenth-century font cover, a painted screen and carvings of wild men on the misericords.

Norwich Cathedral: Most Holy and Undivided Trinity. Enquiries: telephone 0603 626290.

This cathedral is one of the great Norman buildings of England. It was started by Bishop Losinga in 1096 and the main structure was completed by his successors before the end of the twelfth century. Later bishops replaced the original timber roofs and spire and added windows in the Gothic style. The cathedral stands in a beautiful close alongside the ruins of the Benedictine monastery (see page 80), and its tall spire dominates the city. Some points of distinction are the Anglo-Saxon consecration stones below the Bishop's throne; the ancient design of the apse with a walkway round the high chancel and radiating chapels; the seven hundred carved roof bosses and the carved misericords telling stories from Christian mythology and history, and also depicting everyday life in medieval and Tudor times. The medieval painted reredos in St Luke's Chapel is another of the cathedral's treasures. It is hard to imagine that this quiet and orderly cathedral was once brightly coloured and resounded to the singing of huge choirs and the sounding of trumpets or that there were fires, wilful destruction, pillaging and musket fire within its walls. There is much history to discover and beauty to enjoy. The cathedral shop sells guides, and tours and films are available.

Norwich: Friends' Meeting House (Quakers), Upper Goat Lane, Norwich NR2 1EW.

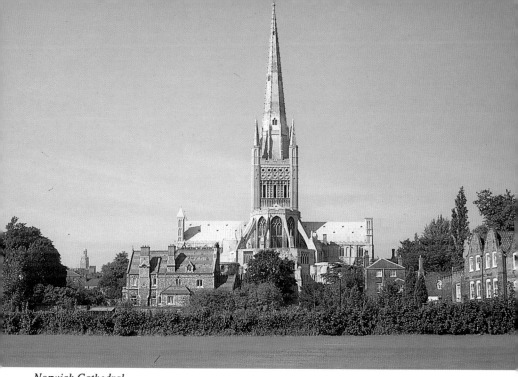

Norwich Cathedral.

Norwich Cathedral cloisters.

Telephone: 0603 624854.

Elizabeth Fry, one of the eleven children of John Gurney, the Norwich banker, worshipped here and in an earlier meeting house which stood on the site. The present meeting house was built in 1826 of grey brick. It has an imposing frontage with two pairs of Doric columns flanking the entrance and projecting wings enclosing a pretty courtyard. Visitors are welcome.

Norwich: The Octagon Chapel (Unitarian).

This octagonal chapel was built in 1753 by Thomas Ivory and was described by John Wesley as 'the most elegant meeting house in Europe'. The inside is as handsome as the exterior, with eight Corinthian columns supporting wooden galleries.

Norwich: Old Meeting House, Colegate (Congregational).

This was built in red brick in 1693 and decorated with flat pilasters surmounted by carved capitals. It has the earliest sash windows in Norwich and the original interior has been preserved.

Norwich: St Giles.

The tower of this church is the tallest in Norwich and the fourteenth-century church presents a fine picture standing in a pretty churchyard with wistaria tumbling over the churchyard walls. Inside, there is a beautiful roof with angels, a carved font, interesting monuments and an ancient parish chest.

Norwich: St John the Baptist Cathedral (Roman Catholic).

This imposing church was built around 1900 for the fifteenth Duke of Norfolk in the Early English style, unusual in a city of churches mainly in later Gothic styles. The spacious but rather gloomy interior is relieved by the fine stained glass windows in the style of the thirteenth century.

Norwich: St Julian.

The fourteenth-century mystic Mother Julian of Norwich almost certainly took her name from this church. The present building was erected in 1953, the ancient church having been destroyed in the Second World War, and it has become a centre for the study of Mother Julian's works and the promotion of contemplative prayer.

Norwich: St Mary Coslany.

The round tower of this church is Anglo-Saxon, the rest Perpendicular. Its greatest glory is the timber roof with carvings of angels and the Virgin.

Norwich: St Michael (Miles) at Coslany.

The fifteenth-century flushwork decoration on the walls of the chancel and south aisle is worth seeing. The doorways are elaborately carved and were the subject of a painting by Cotman.

Norwich: St Peter Mancroft (correctly St Peter and St Paul).

This is the most admired of Norwich churches and one of the finest in England. It was built between 1390 and 1523, replacing an earlier church, and its size and the rich detail of the design give it the majesty and prestige befitting the merchant church of a great city. The unbroken roof and seventeen clerestory windows are best seen from the market. Notice also the massive and highly decorated tower, which has a passage through it to allow processions to pass. Inside, the church is just as impressive. The bells of the church were once pealed to celebrate the defeat of the Spanish Armada. There is a display of church plate, documents and other treasures.

Oxborough: St John the Evangelist.

The nave was destroyed when the medieval stone tower and spire fell in 1948. A fine Perpendicular window containing some medieval glass lights the church, which has a fine roof and piscina and sedilia. But the chief feature here is the Bedingfield Chantry adjoining the church which has two rare sixteenth-century terracotta tombs and other interesting monuments.

Pulham St Mary: St Mary the Virgin.

The tall tower and the elaborate fifteenth-century south porch of this village church in the Waveney valley are very fine. The interior, including the screen, was well restored in 1886. In the chancel there is a thirteenth-century piscina with interlacing arches.

Ranworth: St Helen.

Ranworth church has some of the finest Christian art treasures in England. The painted screen has twelve saints and other figures painted on the wings and side panels. It is thought to be the work of local artists in the fifteenth century. The church also owns the Sarum Antiphoner (1400), a service book written and illuminated by the monks of Langley Abbey and given to Ranworth church in 1478. Six old stalls may have come from nearby St Benet's Abbey (see page 81). There are good views from the tower, which is usually open to the public.

Reepham: St Mary (St Michael's, Whitwell, and All Saints', Hackford, are in the same churchyard).

This is probably a unique example of three churches in one churchyard; two are still in use but of the third only a few walls remain. Each had its own parish, the boundaries of which met in the churchyard, where a cross once stood. The remains of this white stone cross can be seen in St Mary's. It has figures of the Virgin and St John peeping below the cross piece. In St Mary's there is also a tomb to Sir Hugh Kerdiston (1377), depicted lying on a bed of stones, and a brass to Sir William de Kerdiston and his wife.

Salle: St Peter and St Paul.

The pinnacles of the tall flint tower of this magnificent church can be seen from afar across the fields. It was built for rich wool merchants and the story of the church is told in the modern stained glass window in the north transept. There are censing angels above the west doorway, and the interior, with its simple architectural forms and exciting details, is stunning. There are

Left: *Interior of the church of St Peter Mancroft, Norwich.*
Right: *Part of the painted screen at Ranworth church.*

The effigy of the Swaffham pedlar in the church of St Peter and St Paul in Swaffham.

Opposite: *Terracotta work in the chantry chapel of Oxborough church.*

Salle church.

carved and painted angels in the roof, a Seven Sacraments font, carvings on the stalls and misericords, medieval stained glass and interesting brasses. Salle is pronounced 'Saul'.

Shelton: St Mary.
Very late Gothic churches are rare in Norfolk and this is a fine example. It is a rebuilding of an earlier church and was completed in 1487. It has red brick walls with a diaper pattern in darker brick and wide windows, Tudor in style. As a child the future Queen Elizabeth I was sent to Shelton for safety when her mother, Anne Boleyn, was executed. The princess worshipped in this church and for a while was hidden in the tower.

South Burlingham: St Edmund.
Here, almost lost in the countryside, is a charming thatched church which is also a sample book of styles ranging from Norman to Perpendicular. Inside is the finest fifteenth-century pulpit in Norfolk, still with some of the original colouring. There are also medieval carved bench ends and two faded paintings of St Christopher and St Thomas à Becket.

South Lopham: St Andrew.
The Norman tower, embattled and arcaded like a miniature castle, is the finest in Norfolk apart from that of Norwich Cathedral. Much of the rest of the church is also Norman. The late medieval bench ends include a carving of a strange beaked animal with a castle on its back – a fifteenth-century version of an elephant.

Swaffham: St Peter and St Paul.
This beautiful Perpendicular church, built of Barnack stone, has a tower with a spire and grand west window and doorway, a fine south porch and a clerestory of thirteen windows. Inside, the hammerbeam roof of chestnut has two hundred carved angels. There is an effigy of the Swaffham pedlar with his wife and dog in the chancel (see page 50) and the dog also appears on the porch gable.

Terrington St Clement: St Clement.
This 'cathedral of the marshes' is 167 feet (50 metres) long and was built in the fifteenth century of stone. The separate tower which stands alongside, almost touching the south aisle, was built in the early sixteenth century. The west end is particularly fine, with a huge window, niches, pinnacles and gables. The south porch is almost Tudor in style and the chancel clerestory has Tudor brickwork. The font cover opens to reveal paintings of religious scenes set in Renaissance landscapes.

Tilney All Saints: All Saints.
The spire and solid square tower of this lovely church can be seen for miles across the flat fields. It is a Norman church with Perpendicular additions; the long nave with arcades is Norman but the windows and the hammerbeam roof with angels are fifteenth-century. A crusader knight killed at Acre in 1291 was brought back to Tilney for burial and his grave slab can be seen in the north aisle.

Trunch: St Botolph.
This church has all the atmosphere of a medieval church and is built of flint like many of the cottages clustered around it. The font

canopy, one of only four in England of this type, has amazing carvings. Look for a bird pecking grapes, a squirrel with nuts, a pig with a mitre and a monkey with a crozier. Other treasures are the hammerbeam roof and the painted screen.

Tunstead: St Mary.

The church stands away from the village, once a thriving weaving centre with a market, commemorated in Market Street in the village. This imposing church, 140 feet (42 metres) long, was built in the late fourteenth century in a blend of late Gothic styles. It has lofty aisles but instead of clerestory windows there is flushwork arcading. There is a rood screen with twelve painted saints and behind the altar a raised platform, perhaps for the display of relics, with a vault below.

Walpole St Peter: St Peter.

This church was described as 'probably the finest church in England' by Alec Clifton-Taylor and John Betjeman called it 'the finest of them all. It is a masterpiece of fifteenth-century architecture.' Admire the outside first, walking round it and through a passage under the chancel as processions did in medieval times. Inside, the church is filled with light pouring through the Perpendicular windows to reveal a host of fine details: roof bosses, medieval glass, a sixteenth-century font cover that opens, carved benches, stone canopies over the choir stalls, a painted screen and a Jacobean pulpit.

Walsingham: Slipper Chapel, Our Lady of Walsingham (Roman Catholic).

This pretty fourteenth-century building, actually in the village of Houghton St Giles, was in a state of disrepair when it was bought by Miss Charlotte Boyd in 1894. She converted to Roman Catholicism and the chapel was restored and became a Catholic shrine. A modern church has been built nearby, reflecting the local architecture by using flints and echoing the shape of a Norfolk barn.

Walsoken: All Saints.

This stone church with many Norman features stands among trees in a suburb of Wisbech and is only just in Norfolk. Inside, the atmosphere is very Norman: the nave arcades have zigzag decorations, the pillars are alternately round and octagonal, and there are Norman doorways and arches. There are also fine medieval details, such as the Seven Sacraments font and carved stalls and benches.

West Walton: St Mary.

This remarkable church is in the Early English style and built of stone. It was inspired by the churches in Lincolnshire just to the north. The sturdy detached tower stands some distance from the heavily buttressed church, both facts reflecting the problems of subsidence that marshland churches face. The interior is stunning, especially the ranks of pillars with stiffly carved foliage at the base and clusters of eight slim Purbeck limestone shafts attached to each.

Wiggenhall St Mary the Virgin: St Mary the Virgin.

This white rendered church nestling among trees is redundant but well worth a visit. The carved bench ends have saints in niches (sixteenth-century), said to be the finest in England. Other treasures include the alabaster tomb of Sir Henry Kervil, who died in 1624.

He is shown in full armour, with his wife. The octagonal font cover is topped with a pelican. The other two Wiggenhall churches, St German's (Germaine's) and St Mary Magdalen, are also among the finest in Marshland.

A medieval version of an elephant from a bench end at South Lopham church.

Great Bircham Windmill.

Wolterton Hall Gardens.

Wilby: All Saints.

In 1633 a fire destroyed the roof, seating and timberwork of the steeple of this tiny church. The Wilby carpenter was employed to construct the somewhat rustic pews, a fine three-decker pulpit, an altar table and altar rails. This Jacobean furniture, in pale seasoned timber, is most attractive. The church itself is fourteenth-century.

Worstead: St Mary.

The wonderful 109 foot (32 metre) high tower of this Perpendicular church looks across the village square towards the houses and cottages of the weavers and merchants who provided the wealth to build it. Inside the church, looms stand in the north aisle, and weavers will be found at work on them during the annual Worstead Festival in July. The church has a beautiful rood screen with painted saints.

Wymondham: St Mary and St Thomas of Canterbury.

The abbey church (see page 83) was begun in 1107. At the Dissolution the monastery was pulled down and the Norman nave with its beautiful Gothic additions became the parish church and has been considerably embellished since. Both the monks' tower at the east end and the western tower built by the townspeople in 1400 remain, giving the church its distinctive outline. The interior is most impressive with its ranks of arches and windows soaring up to the beautiful hammerbeam roof. There is a modern gilded reredos by Sir Ninian Comper, who also designed the rood and tester.

Wymondham church.

8
Historic buildings and gardens

Alby Gardens, Cromer Road, Alby, Erpingham, Norwich NR11 7QE. Telephone: 0263 761590, or 761226 (evenings).
Open Easter to end of September daily except Mondays including bank holidays.

Water gardens and a bee garden as well as more conventional borders and shrubberies have been laid out alongside the craft centre.

Augustine Steward's House, 14 Tombland, Norwich. Telephone: 0603 619056.

Augustine Steward was Mayor of Norwich and its member of Parliament in the sixteenth century and this fine timber-framed house was his home. It is said to have served as the headquarters of the troops called to put down Kett's rebellion in 1549. It has an overhang, carved window shutters and an underpass to St George's yard.

Beeston Hall and Gardens, Beeston St Lawrence, Norwich NR12 8YS. Telephone: 0692 630771.
Open Easter to mid September on Fridays and Sundays, also bank holiday Mondays and Sundays, and Wednesdays in August.

The Preston family have lived here since 1640 but the present house, of squared flint in the Gothick style, was built in the eighteenth century by Jacob Preston, who decided that the old manor house and grounds should be 'improved'. The elegant interior reflects the changing tastes of the family through the years. The park, once landscaped in the Repton manner, has been largely converted to agricultural use but the gardens have been preserved. Teas are served in the orangery and there are wine cellars to inspect.

Blakeney Guildhall, High Street, Blakeney (OS 133: TG 030441). English Heritage.

Open dawn to dusk daily.

The remains of this fourteenth-century building, which was probably a merchant's house, include an interesting brick-vaulted undercroft.

Blickling Hall, Blickling, Aylsham NR11 6NF. Telephone: 0263 733084. National Trust.
Open end of March to end of October daily except Mondays, Thursdays and Good Friday. Open bank holiday Monday. Garden open same days as house and also daily in July and August.

This superb Jacobean house is surrounded by a handsome park and fine gardens. It was the last great house to be built in Norfolk in the Jacobean style, between 1616 and 1627. It was built by Sir Henry Hobart in rich red brick, thought to have been ruddled, or painted an even brighter red, originally. Earlier the Boleyn family had a manor house here and Anne Boleyn, the second queen of Henry VIII, may have lived at Blickling as a girl. The Jacobean house we see today was partly rebuilt in 1767, the front retaining its Jacobean features, but the rest was largely remodelled in the classical style. Most of the principal rooms of this grand house are open to the public, including the long gallery, which has a Jacobean plasterwork ceiling, and a state bedroom. Important furniture, tapestries and pictures are among the original contents of the house on display.

The gardens at Blickling have remarkable herbaceous borders, each based on one colour, and the walk to the Tuscan temple is a blaze of colour in early summer when the rhododendrons and azaleas are in bloom. The bluebell walks are another delight and it is worth seeking out the 'secret' garden, much

Blickling Hall.

loved by the late owner, the eleventh Marquis of Lothian, who gave the estate to the National Trust. There are also an eighteenth-century orangery and a mausoleum in the park.

Bressingham Gardens, Bressingham, Diss IP22 2AB. Telephone: 037988 382 or 386.
Open daily 1st April to mid October.
The garden has 6 acres (2.4 hectares) of alpines, heathers, conifers and perennial plants. The hardy plant nursery can be seen from the steam-hauled train, which is one of the attractions at Bressingham (see page 104). Facilities include a picnic area, restaurants serving teas and lunches, a shop and a plant centre.

Churchman House, at junction of Bethel Street and St Giles, Norwich. Norwich City Council.
Opened by special arrangement: consult the Tourist Information Centre (see page 141).
Built in the middle of the eighteenth century, this is one of the best provincial houses of its period, with fine interior plasterwork, wall paintings and fireplaces.

Dragon Hall, 115-23 King Street, Norwich NR1 1QE. Telephone: 0603 663922. Norfolk and Norwich Heritage Trust.

Open 1st April to end of November, Mondays to Saturdays, and Mondays to Fridays 1st December to end of March, but closed 19th December to 2nd January, bank holiday Mondays and Good Friday.
The hall dates from the fourteenth and fifteenth centuries and belonged to Robert Toppes, a wealthy city merchant, and later to Anne Boleyn's grandfather. The building has had a chequered history; in its latter years it was divided and the parts used as a vicarage, a pub and a butcher's shop. It has been restored by the Norfolk and Norwich Heritage Trust. During restoration a great hall with impressive roof timbers and a delicately carved dragon in one of the spandrels was discovered, hence the name of the hall.

Fairhaven Garden Trust, South Walsham. Warden: 2 The Woodland, Wymers Lane, South Walsham, Norwich NR13 6EA. Telephone: 060549 449.
Open over Easter and in the summer from May to September from Wednesdays to Sundays and on Bank Holidays. Walks with the Warden on Sunday afternoons in July (booking required).
Primulas and rhododendrons are a speciality at these gardens, best seen in early sum-

mer. There are attractive walks through woodland with picturesque bridges over the water gardens.

Felbrigg Hall, Cromer NR11 8PR. Telephone: 026375 444. National Trust.
Open end of March to end of October daily except Tuesdays and Fridays.

This fine seventeenth-century house is hidden deep within Felbrigg Park. It was built for Thomas Windham around 1620 and enlarged in the seventeenth and eighteenth centuries. The estate was bequeathed to the National Trust by a descendant of the Windhams, the historian Wyndham Ketton Cremer. The house has a fine seventeenth-century plaster ceiling showing game birds and the fruits of the table. The wealthy Windhams of the eighteenth century filled the house with fine furniture and china, an outstanding library and pictures collected on the Grand Tour. The collection of stuffed birds in a passage and copper pans in the kitchen strike a more homely note. In the grounds there is an eighteenth-century orangery and in the walled garden a restored dovecote and herb garden.

Glavenside, Letheringsett, Holt NR25 7AR. Telephone: 0263 713181.

The river Glaven flows from the watermill through 4 acres (1.6 hectares) of lawns, water gardens, alpine gardens and a rose garden. There is also a kitchen garden irrigated by a 1903 hydraulic ram. Facilities include restaurants, shop and picnic area.

Gooderstone Water Gardens, Crow Hall Farm, Gooderstone, King's Lynn. Telephone: 036621 645.
Open daily 1st April to end of October.

More than 7 acres (2.8 hectares) of gardens have been created from marshland; artificial ponds and waterways have been dug out and miniature bridges built across the streams.

Hales Hall and Gardens, Hales, Loddon NR14 6QW. Telephone: 050846 395.

This is one of the 'lost' houses of Norfolk. It was built in the late fifteenth century but all that remains of the large moated house is the long gatehouse range, and the great barn (1478), which has stepped gables. The garden is being restored and there are unusual plants for sale.

Holkham Hall and Gardens, Holkham, Wells-next-the-Sea NR23 1AB. Telephone: 0328 710227.

Felbrigg Hall.

Open Easter and bank holiday weekends and end of May to end of September, Sundays to Thursdays.

Holkham is the grand house of our imagination, grand in its classical design, richly furnished, the seat of a noble family (the Cokes and Earls of Leicester) and the centre of a great estate. The hall was designed by William Kent for Sir Thomas Coke, later first Earl of Leicester, and built in the middle of the eighteenth century from light grey bricks made on the estate to imitate stone. The house owes its inspiration to Sir Thomas's Grand Tour and the reception rooms and state bedrooms are full of fine furniture, tapestries, paintings and beautiful objects. In the grounds there are avenues of ilex and beech first planted in 1729, a monument to Coke of Norfolk (the agricultural reformer), a large lake, an obelisk, a temple, a conservatory, a great barn and a model farm. In the outhouses there are museum displays, a pottery and tea rooms. The house was open to visitors as long ago as the eighteenth century.

Houghton Hall, Houghton, King's Lynn PE31 6UE. Telephone: 0485 528569.
Open Easter to last weekend in September on Thursdays, Sundays and bank holiday Mondays.

Houghton Hall is considered by many to be Norfolk's finest house. It was built by Sir Robert Walpole, the first Prime Minister of Great Britain, in 1721 in creamy Yorkshire stone in the new Palladian style. The interiors are equally magnificent and were designed by William Kent for entertaining on a grand scale. Silk and velvet hangings, tapestries, gilding and marble create a rich background for the fine eighteenth-century furniture and a collection of paintings by such masters as Zoffany, Oudry, Reynolds and Kneller. In the twentieth century the house has been restored by the fifth Marquess of Cholmondeley, a descendant of Sir Robert Walpole, and the Dowager Lady Cholmondeley, who has added treasures from her own family. Houghton also has a very good collection of some twenty thousand model soldiers and militaria, stables with horses and Shetland ponies, a picnic area and an extensive deer park. There is a gift shop, cafeteria, picnic area and childen's playground.

Hoveton Hall Gardens, Hoveton, Norwich NR12 8RJ. Telephone: 0603 782798.
Open Easter to mid September on Wednesdays, Fridays, Sundays and bank holidays in the afternoons.

The 10 acres (4 hectares) of gardens in a woodland setting provide interesting and instructive walks. There is also a lake, a walled herbaceous garden and a Victorian kitchen garden. The garden is especially good for daffodils, azaleas and rhododendrons.

Mannington Gardens and Countryside, Mannington Hall, Saxthorpe, Norwich NR11 7BB. Telephone: 026387 284.
Gardens open first weekend in April to end of October on Sunday afternoons and from early May to end of August also on Wednesdays, Thursdays and Fridays, late morning and afternoons. The house is open only by prior arrangement to specialist groups.

This is one of the few surviving medieval houses in Norfolk, and in spite of nineteenth-century alterations and additions it retains the shape and atmosphere of a moated manor. The flint walls are decorated with terracotta work; there are leaded windows, turrets and battlements. The house is surrounded by a 20 acre (8 hectare) park with a lake, horses' graveyard, a temple and a Saxon chapel. An acre (0.4 hectare) of walled kitchen garden is filled with over a thousand roses. The gardens are open to the public and there are 20 miles (32 km) of waymarked walks through beautiful countryside (see page 58).

Medieval Merchant's House, 9 King Street, King's Lynn PE30 1ET. Telephone: 0553 772545.

Behind the eighteenth-century façade of this house are many features from earlier centuries, such as the pointed-arch window at the rear and Tudor beams and fireplaces. The house has a collection of seventeenth-century maps and Kaufman prints.

Old Merchant's House and Row 111 Houses, South Quay, Great Yarmouth NR30

2RG. Telephone: 0493 887900. English Heritage.
Open April to end of September daily; admission by tour only.

These are seventeenth-century houses which have been restored by English Heritage and now house a collection of local architectural and domestic fittings. Also on South Quay (number 4) is the Elizabethan House, owned by the National Trust but used as a museum (see page 106).

Oxburgh Hall and Gardens, Oxborough, King's Lynn PE33 9PS. Telephone: 036621 258. National Trust.
Open last weekend in March to end of October from Saturdays to Wednesdays in the afternoons and also on bank holiday Mondays.

It is something of a miracle that this fifteenth-century fortified manor house, built of red brick, has survived to the present day. The house was presented to the National Trust by the Roman Catholic Bedingfield family, who had owned it since it was built. Here Mary, Queen of Scots, was imprisoned (her embroidery is on show), Roman Catholic priests were hidden in times of persecution and during the Civil War the house was besieged, pillaged and set on fire by the Parliamentarians. The Tudor gatehouse and the chapel by Pugin are particularly admired. The contents of the house range in style from medieval to Victorian and there is an interesting display of Catholic mementoes. Attractive borders and a French parterre garden surround the moat.

The Pleasaunce, Harbord Road, Overstrand, near Cromer. Telephone: 026378 212.
Open June to September, Monday, Wednesday and Thursday afternoons.

The house was designed by Lutyens and the gardens by Gertrude Jekyll. It is now a Christian centre. Teas are served.

Rainthorpe Hall and Gardens, Tasburgh, Norwich NR15 1RQ. Telephone: 0508 470618.
Open from the end of March to the end of October on Wednesdays, Saturdays, Sundays and bank holidays all day.

This timbered Elizabethan house has beautiful brickwork with blue diapering and the contents include medieval stained glass, part of a Gothic rood screen collected by a previous owner and fine period furniture. The handsome trees and the collection of bamboos in the garden are of interest, and there is a medieval nuttery and an Elizabethan knot garden. The interior of the house can be seen by appointment only, all year round.

Raveningham Gardens, near Loddon, Norwich NR1 6NS. Telephone: 0508 46206.
Open Sundays and bank holidays in the afternoons from the end of March to mid September.

This is a real country-house garden surrounding an elegant Georgian house. It is a plantsman's paradise with interesting and rare species. The nurseries near the garden are open daily.

St George's Guildhall (The Fermoy Centre), King's Street, King's Lynn PE30 1AH. Telephone: 0553 4725. National Trust.
Open all year, Monday to Friday, but closed on Good Friday, bank holiday Mondays, 25th and 26th December and 1st January. Closed Saturday afternoons.

The Guild of St George built this guildhall between 1410 and 1420 and it is the largest surviving building of its kind in England. It is still covered by the original massive timbered roof. The building has long been associated with theatrical productions and there is a tradition that Shakespeare played here; certainly his company is recorded as doing so. The King's Lynn Festival, held annually in July, takes place here.

Sandringham House, Grounds, Museum and Country Park, Sandringham, King's Lynn PE35 6EN. Telephone: 0553 772675.
House, grounds, country park and museum open except when the Queen or any member of the Royal Family is in residence. Telephone to check times.

In 1861 the Prince of Wales (later King Edward VII) decided to buy the Sandringham estate, having considered estates in other counties. In 1870 a new house was built in the Jacobean style in brick with stone facings, and

Oxburgh Hall.

a second storey and other embellishments were added in 1891. Sandringham is popular with the Royal Family and crowds gather to watch them on their way to and from church when the Queen is in residence. The grounds are most attractive. Sandringham Flower Show is held each year on the last Wednesday in July.

Sheringham Park, Upper Sheringham. Telephone (Warden): 0263 623778. National Trust.

This beautiful 90 acre (36 hectare) park was acquired by the National Trust in 1987. The house and park were designed by Repton in 1812 and are considered to be his finest work. A gazebo has been constructed on the highest point in the park, offering fine views over the coast and countryside. The rhododendron and azalea walks are at their best in early summer. The car park is through the south entrance on the A148 Cromer to Holt road.

Thetford Warren Lodge (OS 144: TL 839841). 2 miles (3 km) north-west of Thetford on the B1107 Brandon road. English Heritage.

In the middle ages rabbits were farmed in Breckland on a large scale and so valuable were the 'coneys' (as rabbits are known in Norfolk) that fortified lodges were built to house the warrener and to serve as a strong-room for the rabbit meat and skins. The warren lodge at Thetford is the best-preserved of all the medieval lodges. It can be viewed from the outside.

Wolterton Hall Gardens, Erpingham, Norwich NR11 7LY. Telephone (estate office): 026377 274.
The rose garden, herbaceous borders, parkland and lake are open to the public on advertised days but the house is open only to organisations making advance bookings.

G. S. Repton, the son of Humphry Repton, was commissioned to remodel the hall, which had been built a century earlier by Horatio Walpole, and also to landscape the garden.

9
Museums and art galleries

Alby

Lace Museum and Study Centre and Bottle Museum. See Alby Craft Centre, page 125.

Bressingham

Bressingham Live Steam Museum, Bressingham, Diss IP22 2AB. Telephone: 0379 888133.

Open daily April to October inclusive. Steam days Sundays, Thursdays and bank holiday Mondays, also Wednesdays in July and August.

Here the visitor can enjoy a complete experience of the age of steam. There are more than fifty steam engines of various types, including the famous railway locomotive *Royal Scot.* Visitors can ride on one of the steam-hauled trains along 5 miles (8 km) of narrow-gauge railways through woodlands and gardens. Another attraction is the steam-operated Victorian roundabout. The museum is part of the Bressingham Gardens complex (see page 99).

Burston

Burston Strike School Museum, Burston, Diss IP22 3TP. Custodian: M. W. Philpot, 8 Shreeves Road, Diss IP22 3HO. Telephone: 0379 652659 or 741565.

Opened on request; key available in village.

The museum is housed in the building erected to provide classrooms for children of the strike school. The displays include documents, photographs and objects related to the strike.

Caister-on-Sea

Caister Castle Car Collection. See Caister Castle, page 78.

Cockley Cley

Iceni Village and Museum. See page 125.

Cockthorpe

Cockthorpe Hall Toy Museum, Cockthorpe, Wells-next-the-Sea NR23 1OS. Telephone: 0328 830293.

Open daily.

Model trains, mechanical toys, dolls, toy animals and dolls' houses are exhibited in this museum in a sixteenth-century house.

Cromer

Cromer Museum, East Cottages, Tucker Street, Cromer NR27 9HB. Telephone: 0263 513543. Norfolk Museums Service.

Open daily; afternoons only on Sundays. Closed Good Friday and 24th to 26th December.

This excellent museum has been set up in a terrace of five Victorian fishermen's cottages, one of which has been furnished as it would have been just before the First World War. There are models of a fisherman and his wife in their cramped kitchen, which like the rest of the cottage has been furnished with authentic items provided by local people. There are also displays illustrating the archaeology, history, geology and natural history of north Norfolk. Collections of local bygones such as Poppyland china, tourist posters and photographs of Cromer in Victorian and Edwardian days are on show, and from time to time there are demonstrations of local skills such as crab-pot making and fishermen's knitting. A local studies collection can be seen by appointment.

The Old Boathouse Lifeboat Museum, The Slipway, Cromer.

Open daily May to September inclusive.

The lifeboat museum is situated on the sea front at the southern end of the promenade. It has fascinating models, paintings, photographs and mementoes which tell the story of the lifeboats and lifeboatmen of the past. The lifeboat house at the end of the pier is also open to the public and the lifeboats *Ruby* and

Bishop Bonner Cottages Museum, East Dereham.

Arthur Read II can be seen (telephone: 0263 512237).

Diss
Diss Museum, Market Place, Diss IP22 3AB. For information telephone Mrs Flatman: 0379 642014.
Open Wednesday afternoon and all day Friday; also Saturdays and Bank Holidays in summer and Sunday afternoons.

This is a small museum, housed in part of a shop, which has an interesting collection of old photographs of the town.

East Dereham
Bishop Bonner Cottages Museum, St Withburga Lane, East Dereham NR19 1ED. Telephone: 0362 693107.
Open afternoons, Tuesdays to Saturdays in the summer.

This thatched cottage, dating back to 1502, makes a fitting home for a museum of local history. The front of the cottage has a frieze of pargeting – unusual in Norfolk – with a design of roses, vine leaves and stars. There are displays of local domestic utensils, and agricultural bygones, a small archaeological section and mementoes of Dereham's men of letters, William Cowper, George Borrow and Dr Jessop.

Fakenham
Fakenham Museum of Gas and Local History. See page 115.

Forncett St Mary
Industrial Steam Museum, Low Road. Forncett St Mary, Norwich NR16 1JJ. Telephone: 050841 8277.
Open for steam days: the first Sunday in each month May to December.

The museum houses an extensive collection of large stationary steam engines, the biggest being an 85 ton triple expansion engine from Dover waterworks and the oldest an 1873 lace-mill engine. The best-known exhibit is the Vickers compound engine used to open Tower Bridge until 1974. The museum gives a fascinating reminder of how stationary steam engines supplied the power to drive factories, waterworks, dairies, laundries, breweries, maltings and many other applications, from the mid nineteenth century until recent times. On advertised steam days eight engines are run.

Great Yarmouth

Elizabethan House Museum, 4 South Quay, Great Yarmouth NR30 2SH. Telephone: 0493 855746. Norfolk Museums Service and National Trust.
Open daily in summer, except Saturdays.

Behind the Georgian façade of this building is a merchant's house built in 1596 with panelled rooms, decorative plaster ceilings and contemporary furniture. Other rooms in the house are used to display Yarmouth souvenirs, Lowestoft china, early kitchen equipment, Victorian toys and other items illustrating the social history of the town. There is also a good collection of paintings, many of local scenes.

Lydia Eva Steam Drifter, Town Quay, Great Yarmouth.
Open daily July to October (and at Lowestoft from Easter to June).

The *Lydia Eva* was one of the last steam drifters to be built. Now she is the last of over three thousand drifters that came to Yarmouth every autumn to fish for herring. Displays on board show the hardships suffered by the fishermen aboard and on shore.

Maritime Museum for East Anglia, 25 Marine Parade, Great Yarmouth NR30 2EN. Telephone: 0493 842267.
Open daily in summer, except Saturdays.

This museum is housed in a former home for shipwrecked sailors and has extensive displays covering every aspect of Norfolk's rich maritime history. There are models of ships, displays of navigational and lifesaving aids, shipbuilding, fishing and sailors' crafts.

Tolhouse Museum and Brass Rubbing Centre, Tolhouse Street, Great Yarmouth NR30 2SQ. Telephone: 0493 858900.
Open daily in summer, except Saturdays.

The Tolhouse is one of England's oldest municipal buildings, dating back to the thirteenth century. It once served as a courthouse and jail and the dungeons with their original cells may be visited. There are displays on three floors illustrating the history of the district from Roman times to the Second World War.

Tolhouse Museum, Great Yarmouth.

The Norfolk Rural Life Museum at Gressenhall.

Gressenhall

Norfolk Rural Life Museum, Beech House.
Gressenhall, East Dereham NR20 4DR. Telephone: 0362 860563. Norfolk Museums Service.

Open April to October, Tuesdays to Saturdays all day and Sunday afternoons.

Every aspect of rural life since the eighteenth century is imaginatively displayed here, from farm machinery to domestic life. The museum building was once a workhouse. In the outhouses there are reconstructions of rural workshops such as a saddler's shop and a blacksmith's forge. Cherry Tree Cottage is a typical farmworker's home of the early twentieth century and the garden is stocked with old-fashioned flowers and vegetables. Special exhibitions, events and children's activities are held throughout the season. There is a picnic area in the museum grounds.

Holkham

Bygones at Holkham, Holkham Park, Wells-next-the-Sea NR23 1AB. Telephone: 0328 710806.

Open May to September daily, also bank holiday Sundays and Mondays.

This bygones museum includes displays of fire engines, farming implements, cars and traction engines, and there are workshop reconstructions of the domestic and estate activities that were part of the life of a great house such as Holkham. During the summer there are craft demonstrations and days when the steam engines are in steam.

King's Lynn

The Fermoy Centre, King Street, King's Lynn PE30 1ET. Telephone: 0553 773578.

Open Mondays to Saturdays all year.

The fifteenth-century St George's Guildhall (see page 102) is the principal building of this arts centre, which occupies a range of medieval buildings. The centre includes a theatre, two galleries and a museum. The prestigious King's Lynn Festival is held here each July.

Lynn Museum, Market Street, King's Lynn PE30 1NL. Telephone: 0553 775001. Norfolk Museums Service.

Open Mondays to Saturdays all year; closed bank holidays.

The history, archaeology, natural history and geology of King's Lynn and west Norfolk are illustrated in this museum. Displays include artefacts from the stone age, iron age and Roman times through Lynn's illustrious history as a trading centre in the middle ages to more recent industries such as whaling, fishing and fairground engineering. Local wildlife is explored through a study of the

Trinity Guildhall and Town House Museum of Lynn Life.

variety of habitats in the area.

Old Gaol House Museum, Regalia Rooms and Heritage Centre, Trinity Guildhall, Saturday Market Place, King's Lynn PE30 1HY. Telephone: 0553 763044.
Open daily in summer, and Tuesdays to Fridays from November to Spring Bank Holiday.

Treasures of Lynn, including the famous fourteenth-century 'King John Cup' and civic regalia, are displayed in the undercroft of the Trinity Guildhall, with a heritage exhibition depicting the town's long history.

The museum building originally housed the town jail and the prison cells can be visited. An audio tour and sound and light effects bring to life stories of some of Lynn's most notorious criminals.

Town House Museum of Lynn Life, 46 Queen Street, King's Lynn PE30 5DQ (next to the Town Hall). Telephone: 0553 773450. Norfolk Museums Service.

The way of life of Lynn's merchants,

tradespeople and their families comes alive in the historic room displays, which include exhibits of costume and toys. There is also a reconstruction of a working Victorian kitchen and a 1950s sitting room.

True's Yard, North Street, King's Lynn PE30 1QW. Telephone: 0553 770479.
Open daily all year, except Fridays from November to February.

The fishing community of Lynn is celebrated in this heritage centre set up in the only remaining fishermen's yard in the county. It includes a museum and restored cottages. There are displays and demonstrations of the skills of the fishermen and their wives, and facilities for the study of maritime and fishing history.

Little Dunham

Dunham Museum, Station House, Little Dunham, King's Lynn PE32 2EJ. Telephone: 0760 23073.
Open daily from April to September.

The tools and machinery used by traditional rural craftsmen and utensils from the dairy and kitchen are among the bygones exhibited in this museum

North Creake

The Forge Museum, Church Street, North Creake, Fakenham NR21 9AD. Telephone: 0328 738910.

Open daily Easter to end of September.

This working forge museum also has a small display of village bygones. Ironwork from the forge made by traditional methods is on sale.

North Elmham

County School Station Museum, North Elmham.

Open Saturdays and Sundays all the year and on bank holidays.

This country railway station 5 miles (8 km) north of East Dereham has been restored. There is also a short length of track and a diesel train and brake-van. An exhibition has displays on the railway, the County School and the Wensum valley. Nearby are a picnic area and waymarked circular walks.

Norwich

Bridewell Museum of Norwich Trades and Industries, Bridewell Alley, Norwich NR2 1AQ. Telephone: 0603 667228. Norfolk Museums Service.

Open all year, Mondays to Saturdays.

The Bridewell, as its name suggests, was once a prison but before that, in the fourteenth century, it was the home of a mayor of Norwich. Now it is a museum of local trades and industries since the eighteenth century. There is a collection of locally made clocks, reconstructions of a blacksmith's forge, a chemist's shop of the early twentieth century and a Victorian bar. Other displays tell the story of weaving and other local industries.

Castle Museum, Norwich NR1 3JU. Telephone: 0603 223624, extension 24. Norfolk Museums Service.

Open Monday to Saturdays, and Sunday afternoons.

The Norman castle opened as a museum in 1894 and is one of the finest regional museums in Britain. The keep forms an ideal setting for historical displays of medieval objects, armour, Egyptian mummies and an exhibit illustrating the links between Norfolk and Europe. Other galleries contain displays of natural history, archaeology, social history and ceramics, including a collection of Lowestoft ware and one of teapots. There is a display of pages from the diary of Margaret Fountaine, the lepidopterist. Paintings by the Norwich School of artists are on show. There are tours of the dungeons and battlements.

City of Norwich Aviation Museum, Old Norwich Road, Horsham St Faith, Norwich NR6 6JA. Telephone: 0603 625309.

Open Sundays throughout the year and on Tuesday and Thursday evenings from April to October.

Displays tell the history of aviation in the locality and include a fine collection of aircraft, engines and equipment. Some of the aircraft cockpits are open to visitors. The museum offers a good vantage point for viewing aircraft using Norwich airport.

City Regalia, Guildhall, Gaol Hill, Norwich NR2 1NF. Telephone: 0603 666071.

Open Mondays to Fridays.

The regalia include masterpieces of Tudor workmanship.

Norwich Arts Centre, Reeves Yard, St Benedict's Street, Norwich. Telephone: 0603 660352.

Open daily Mondays to Saturdays. Telephone for details of music events.

Photographic exhibitions are a feature of this lively arts centre mainly devoted to jazz, blues, folk and classical concerts and avant-garde theatre.

Norwich Gallery, Norfolk Institute of Art and Design, St George's Street, Norwich. Telephone: 0603 610561.

Open Mondays to Saturdays, and Sunday mornings.

Contemporary art is exhibited here giving tourists an opportunity to purchase interesting pictures.

A figure by Henry Moore at the Sainsbury Centre for the Visual Arts at the University of East Anglia, Norwich.

Royal Norfolk Regimental Museum, Shire Hall, Market Avenue, Norwich NR1 3JQ. Telephone: 0603 223649.
Open daily; afternoons only on Sundays.
This is Norwich's newest museum, housed in the former Crown Courts. It has an entrance in Market Avenue and also can be approached through the old prisoners' tunnel from the Castle. Exhibits tell the story of the Royal Norfolk Regiment in peace and war, including their service in Afghanistan, North and South America and India.

Sainsbury Centre for Visual Arts, University of East Anglia, Norwich NR4 7TJ. Telephone: 0603 56060.
Open afternoons all year except on Mondays.
The wide-ranging Robert and Lisa Sainsbury Collection is of international importance, including European and tribal art; Egyptian, Greek, Etruscan and Roman antiquities; medieval and oriental sculpture; Indian and Japanese painting. Artists represented include Degas, Epstein, Picasso, Modigliani, Arp, Moore, Giacometti and Bacon. The centre also houses the Anderson Collection of art nouveau.

St Peter Hungate Church Museum, Elm Hill, Norwich NR3 1MN. Telephone: 0603 667231. Norfolk Museums Service.
Open Mondays to Saturdays.
Many treasures from redundant churches have found a home here in this beautiful fifteenth-century flint church. The exhibits include medieval illuminated books, church plate, stone and wood carvings, vestments, church music, musical instruments and ironwork. There is also a brass-rubbing centre.

Strangers' Hall Museum, Charing Cross, Norwich NR2 4AL. Telephone: 0603 667229. Norfolk Museums Service.
Open Mondays to Saturdays.
For nearly four hundred years from the fourteenth century this building was the home of rich merchants, and the original medieval house has been added to over the years. Now it displays furniture, furnishings, textiles and costume in a series of period rooms. Toys and musical instruments are also on show and behind the scenes there are collections of costume and textiles, including local smocks, which form the basis of special exhibitions.

Ranworth

Broadland Conservation Centre. See page 70.

Seething

Station 146, Seething Aircraft Control Tower, Seething Airfield, Brooke, Norwich. Telephone: 0508 50787.
Open on advertised days in the summer and by appointment.

This renovated USAAF wartime control tower displays the 448th Bomb Group's honour roll and a collection pictures, diaries and stories from veterans of the Second World War who served in the 448th Bomb Group.

Sheringham

Railway Museum, Sheringham Station, Sheringham NR26 8RA. Telephone: 0263 822045.
Open in the summer, Tuesdays to Saturdays, and Sunday afternoons.

North Norfolk's 'Poppy Line' steam railway (see page 116) begins at Sheringham and the station has been partly converted into a museum. Locomotives and rolling stock, railway bygones, a signal box and a model railway are on show. Information boards give details of the history of the line. The railway has been used for television programmes.

Sheringham Museum, Station Road, Sheringham. Telephone: 0263 823317.
Open April to the autumn, daily except Mondays.

Three traditional cottages with net lofts form the museum, which is mainly devoted to the history of Sheringham and the lives of the people who have, for centuries, earned their living from the sea.

Strumpshaw

Strumpshaw Hall Steam Museum, Hall Farm, Low Road, Strumpshaw, Norwich NR13 4HS. Telephone: 0603 714535.
Open daily in the summer, except Saturdays.

Over twenty steam engines in working order, a beam engine and a fairground organ are among the exhibits at this museum. There is also a working steam railway.

Sutton

Sutton Windmill and Broads Museum. See page 123.

Sheringham Museum.

Swaffham

Swaffham Museum, Town Hall, 4 London Street, Swaffham PE37 7DQ. Telephone: 0760 721230.
Open Tuesdays, Thursdays and Saturdays from end of March to October and also Wednesdays and Fridays from the last week in June to the first week in September.

Local history displays include fossils, stone age implements, armour, tools, coins, local china, weapons, costumes and pictures. Regularly changing temporary exhibitions are also held.

Thetford

Ancient House Museum, 21 White Hart Street, Thetford IP24 1AA. Telephone: 0842 752599. Norfolk Museums Service.
Open weekdays and also Sunday afternoons in the summer.

Ancient House dates back to 1500; it is timber-framed and inside there is a beautiful carved ceiling beam. There are displays relating to local history: Grimes Graves, the Saxon town of Thetford, local industries, and documents and mementoes relating to Thomas Paine, the eighteenth-century reformer and supporter of the American revolution. There are also collections of local flora and fauna to illustrate the natural history of the area.

Charles Burrell Museum, Minstergate, Thetford, Norfolk IP24 3DW. Telephone (Thetford Tourist Information): 0842 752599.
Open April to October, Saturdays, Sundays and bank holidays.

Charles Burrell was the founder of a world-famous Thetford company which manufactured steam engines and agricultural machinery from 1770 to 1932. The museum is housed in the former paint shop of the factory and displays examples of Burrell products, photographs of the Burrell family and employees and copies of working drawings. Workshops have been re-created with the original tools and machinery.

Thorpe Abbotts

100th Bomb Group Memorial Museum, Common Road, Dickleburgh, Diss. Curator:

Ancient House Museum, Thetford.

The former railway station at Wolferton, now a museum, was the nearest to the Royal Family's private home at Sandringham and was often used by royalty.

Mr M. Harvey, 11 Castle Hill, Eye, Suffolk IP23 7AP. Telephone: 0379 870837.

Open all year Saturdays, Sundays and bank holidays; also Wednesdays from May to September.

The control tower of the disused airfield has been converted into a museum as a tribute to the Eighth Air Force and 100th Bomb Group of the United States Air Force, stationed here during the Second World War.

Thursford

The Thursford Museum, Thursford, Fakenham NR21 0AS. Telephone: 032877 477.

Open daily, April to October.

This museum claims to have the world's greatest collection of steam road locomotives, showmen's traction engines and plough and barn engines. It also has a collection of mechanical organs and concerts are a regular feature.

Walsingham

Shirehall Museum, Common Place, Little Walsingham NR22 6BP. Telephone: 0328 820510. Norfolk Museums Service.

Open daily, Easter to September, and Saturdays and Sundays in October.

An almost perfectly preserved Georgian courtroom with a prisoners' lock-up is the principal exhibit in this unusual museum. There are also displays illustrating the history of Walsingham as a pilgrimage centre and on the history of the area. The museum houses the local tourist information centre.

Wells-next-the-Sea

Maritime Museum, Old Lifeboat House, The Quay, Wells-next-the-Sea.

Open daily, except Mondays, from April to mid October in the afternoon and on Saturday mornings.

The maritime history of this interesting small port, including fishing, the port, coastguard, lifeboat and bait digging is on display.

West Walton

Fenland Aviation Museum, Bamber's Garden Centre, Old Lynn Road, West Walton PE14 7DA. Telephone: 0945 63996. *Open Saturdays and Sundays in the summer.*

Aviation relics of the Second World War and domestic bygones of the same period are displayed in a museum set up by the Fenland Aircraft Preservation Society.

Weybourne

Muckleburgh Collection, Old Military Camp, Weybourne NR25 7EG. Telephone: 026370 210. *Open daily Easter to October.*

This is one of the largest private displays of tanks, armoured cars, guns and military vehicles in Britain. It is sited on the military camp used in the First and Second World Wars and includes workshops for the repair of vehicles and displays of military memorabilia in covered exhibition halls. There are also adventure playgrounds for children.

Wolferton

Wolferton Station Museum, Wolferton, King's Lynn PE31 6HA. Telephone: 0485

540674. *Open from Easter to September, Monday to Saturday, and on Sunday afternoons.*

When the Prince of Wales bought Sandringham in 1863 he brought his bride to Norfolk by train to Wolferton, the nearest station. For over one hundred years the Royal Family used the station and the Down Side Royal Retiring Rooms were specially built for them. As well as the rooms set aside for the king and for the queen, the museum has other royal exhibits and relics associated with the Lynn and Hunstanton line.

Wymondham

Wymondham Heritage Museum, 14a Middleton Street, Wymondham NR18 0AD. For information telephone: 0953 603319. *Open Thursday and Friday afternoons and all day Saturdays for most of the summer.*

This is a lively museum which arranges its collection of treasures under different themes each year. The displays are mainly of local and historical interest.

Fakenham Museum of Gas and Local History.

10
Industrial archaeology

Aylsham Navigation

Until the eighteenth century the river Bure was navigable only as far as Horstead Mill (destroyed by fire in 1963), but in 1774 locks were constructed at the mills at Buxton, Oxnead, Burgh-next-Aylsham and Aylsham and the navigation was opened in 1779. From the beginning it was necessary to 'didle' (the Norfolk word for dredging) to maintain the depth of water required by the 13 ton wherries plying the waterway with their cargoes of flour, timber, coal, bricks and other goods. The navigation continued to be used in spite of competition from the railways until the great flood of 1912, which badly damaged the locks. Some of the machinery of the locks can be seen at the mills, except at Buxton where the lock was removed in the course of road widening in 1933. There is a small canalside settlement at Dunkirk, Aylsham (OS 133: TG 200276).

Bure Valley Railway, The Old Station, Norwich Road, Aylsham NR11 6BW. Telephone: 0263 733858.
Open at Easter and daily from June to September.

A 9 mile (14 km) stretch of an old railway line has been relaid on 15 inch (381 mm) gauge and now links Wroxham and the Broads with Aylsham and connects with the National Trust property at Blickling Hall. The trains are powered alternatively by steam and diesel engines. The journey takes forty minutes, passing through typical Norfolk countryside with three halts on the way.

Denver Sluice (OS 143: TF 587009).

The first sluice on the Great Ouse was constructed 2 miles (3 km) west of Denver in 1834 to a design by Sir John Rennie. It has been widened and remodelled since, most recently in 1964, when the Great Denver Sluice was constructed. Until 1966 there was

a toll bridge here and a list of charges and a history of the sluices can be seen at the Jenyns Arms public house. The sluices control the complicated river and tidal conditions and when necessary channel flood water into an overflow channel.

Fakenham Museum of Gas and Local History, Hempton Road, Fakenham (OS 132: TF 918292). Enquiries to: J. G. Ashley, 2 Victoria Lane, Fakenham NR21 8LB. Telephone: 0328 851696. Fakenham Town Gasworks Museum Trust.
Open daily June to mid September, also Easter and May Bank Holiday.

The works, opened in 1846, is the only surviving example in England of the small horizontal-retort hand-fired gasworks and is substantially complete. Much of the equipment dates from the early twentieth century but most of the buildings are nineteenth-century and the gasholder dates from 1888. Unused since closure in 1965, the works has been fully restored. There are displays and an excellent guided tour (by prior arrangement).

Geldeston (Shipmeadow) Tidal Lock (OS 134: TM 908390), near Locks Inn, Geldeston, Norfolk NR34 0HW. Telephone: 050845 414. The lock can be reached by river or along a rough road from Geldeston village.

In 1672 a series of three tidal locks was opened on the Waveney upriver from Beccles in order to extend the navigation to Bungay and enable trading wherries carrying mainly corn, coal and timber to extend their area of operation. The remains of one of the locks can be seen on the Geldeston side of the river. The lock was last in use in 1934. The remains of a staithe, malthouse and large brewery can be seen in the village at the end of the Geldeston Dyke near to the Wherry Inn. The old railway station serving the now defunct

Waveney Valley Line can also be seen. In former times the Locks Inn was the scene of smuggling and elicit deals, disputes and fighting between the wherrymen. The county boundary runs through the lock so that it was easy for the wherrymen to avoid arrest by crossing to another county according to which county constabulary was called.

Gunton Sawmill, Gunton Park, Hanworth (OS 133: TG 224335). Norfolk Mills and Pumps Trust, County Hall, Norwich NR1 2DH. Telephone: 0603 222705.

Lord Suffield of Gunton Hall near Cromer built this sawmill in the 1820s to provide timber for his estate. It is powered by water from an ornamental lake and has two metal breastshot waterwheels, a belt and pulley drive and a large reciprocating frame saw. The mill is housed in a picturesque timber-framed building and has been restored to working order by the Norfolk Windmills Trust, aided by volunteers from the Industrial Archaeology Society. Demonstrations take place on advertised open days.

Melton Constable Locomotive Works and Railway Housing (OS 133: TG 043330 and TG 045330).

This small town on Lord Hastings's estate in north Norfolk was the unlikely choice for a junction and locomotive works of the Midland and Great Northern Railway. The railway line that it served opened in 1887 and closed in 1964. The M&GNR company was never very successful and was jokingly referred to as the Muddle and Get Nowhere line. The workshops at Melton Constable and a few remains of the station can still be seen, including three large water tanks on cast-iron columns. In the town there are terraces of houses and a grander house built for the chief engineer in the typically ornate M&GN style between 1885 and 1910.

North Norfolk Railway, Sheringham Station, Sheringham NR26 8RA. Telephone: 0263 822045; talking timetable 0263 825449.

The old Midland & Great Northern line ran from Cromer to Sheringham, Weybourne, Holt and Melton Constable from 1887 but by

1964 all except the Cromer to Sheringham section had been closed. A preservation society was established and the line has been reopened as the 'Poppy Line' between Sheringham and Holt, with steam trains in operation in the summer, and diesel railbuses throughout the year. There is a 'Santa Special' steam train at Christmas time. At Sheringham station there is also a railway museum (see page 111).

Northrepps Iron Foundry and Sawpit, 21 Church Street, Northrepps, Cromer NR27 0AA. Telephone: 026378 277. *Viewing is by appointment only.*

The foundry of this long-established business belonging to the Golden family is no longer in use but it is complete with its forges, furnaces, casting boxes and nineteenth-century engines intact. There is also one of the few surviving sawpits in Britain and a working sawmill with many interesting tools. There are some horse-drawn vehicles and implements made on the premises, the last generating set used in a rural telephone exchange in Norfolk and a variety of small farm engines.

North Walsham to Dilham Canal

This canal runs for nearly 9 miles (14 km) alongside the river Ant from Antingham near North Walsham to Dilham, to link with the Broads network of waterways. The canal opened in 1825 and the last wherry loaded a cargo of timber at Bacton Wood in December 1934. Because the water was so shallow a small type of wherry was used but silting up was always a problem and the canal never recovered from the damage caused by the 1912 floods. At Antingham the old Barge Inn and the ruins of a bone mill can still be seen, and there are locks in various stages of decay at Swafield, Bacton Wood, Ebridge Mill, Briggate, Honing and Dilham.

Norwich: Carrow Works (OS 134: TG 242075).

J. J. Colman erected a large mustard mill and associated buildings in the second half of the nineteenth century and many parts are still in use.

Norwich: New Mills Pumping Station, off Westwick Street, Norwich (OS 134: TG 226091).

In 1898 a sewage pumping station was erected here to pump sewage to the Trowse treatment plant. The name New Mills dates from the fifteenth century when flour mills were built here across the river Wensum by the city corporation, which had a monopoly of flour milling in the city. An industrial museum is planned for the site.

Norwich Yarn Mill (now Jarrolds' printing works), Whitefriars, Norwich NR3 1SH (OS 134: TG 235093).

This former worsted mill is a handsome six-storey brick building with a domed staircase tower at one end, now covered with creeper. It is inscribed: NORWICH YARN COMPANY 1839. There are other reminders of the weaving industry in Norwich, such as the weavers' windows in Pottergate and Bedford Street and weavers' workshops in Wright's Court and Gurney Court off Magdalen Street.

Potter Heigham Bridge (OS 134: TG 420185).

This is a small narrow bridge of late medieval date over the Thurne.

Reedham Ferry (OS 134: TG 407015).

This ferry, the last chain ferry left on the Broads, was built in 1914 and converted to diesel power in 1951. It carries passengers, cars and light commercial traffic across the river Yare.

Wells and Walsingham Light Railway, Wells-next-the-Sea. Please write for timetable and other information.
Open daily April to end of September.

The old Great Eastern track bed is used in summer for carrying passengers between Wells and Walsingham, a distance of 4 miles (6 km). The last standard-gauge British Rail train ran in 1964 and the line was then dismantled. Narrow-gauge track has since been laid and trains are pulled by a steam locomotive, *Norfolk Hero.*

The medieval bridge at Potter Heigham.

11
Windmills, windpumps and watermills

Once there were no less than 850 windmills and a hundred windpumps in Norfolk. Today there are about fifty still standing which are more or less complete and many others that are picturesque ruins. The Norfolk windmills and windpumps (often loosely called 'mills' although they were not used to grind corn) are mainly high tower mills, with four sails and a top like an upturned boat. Only two post mills – the earlier type of mill – survive, at Garboldisham and Thrigby, and there are also a few open-boarded and trestle windpumps.

The number of watermills has also dramatically declined and now there are no mills left with a continuous history as working mills, although in a few cases milling has been revived to meet the demand for stoneground flour.

The Norfolk Mills and Pumps Trust was formed in 1963 to preserve and restore windmills, windpumps and watermills and it now owns or looks after many of the surviving mills and windpumps. The initials NMPT in the headings of the following entries denote that the mill or pump is cared for by the trust.

For further information on the work of the trust and for details of access to the trust's mills and pumps apply to the Technical Adviser, Norfolk Mills and Pumps Trust, County Hall, Norwich NR1 2SG. Telephone: 0603 222705.

Berney Arms High Mill, Reedham (OS 134: TG 465050). Telephone: 0493 700605. English Heritage. On the river Yare near Breydon Water.
Open daily April to September.
Berney Mill is the tallest windpump on the Broads, with seven storeys; it has also been used for grinding cement clinker. The mill is open in the summer and can be reached by rail (Berney Arms station) or by a long walk over the marshes. There is a small exhibition in the mill.

Billingford Windmill (OS 156: TM 167786). 1 mile (1.6 km) east from Scole on A143. NMPT. (Note: there is another Billingford in Norfolk, near East Dereham, which has a watermill.)
Open all the year round. The keys are available at the Horseshoes public house.
This is a very attractive five-storey red

brick tower mill with a white boat-shaped top, sails and fantail. It was the last Norfolk corn mill to work by wind and was milling until 1956.

Bircham Windmill. See Great Bircham, page 120.

Boardman's Drainage Mill. See How Hill, page 121.

Burnham Overy Windmill (OS 132: TF 838438). 6 miles (10 km) west of Wells-next-the-Sea on A149. National Trust.
Not open to the public.
Visitors to north Norfolk are familiar with this landmark on the coast road. The tower mill is six storeys high, tarred black and has been converted into a house. It was built in 1816 and last worked in 1919. There is another five-storey windmill in the village, on

Burnham Overy Windmill.

the B1155 (TF 842426).

Near the windmills is Burnham Overy Watermill (TF 836436) on the river Burn, also owned by the National Trust. It was built in 1737, gutted by fire in 1959 and carefully rebuilt. Alongside is the Georgian miller's house. Neither is open to the public.

Buxton Watermill, Buxton, Norfolk NR10 5JF (OS 134: TG 238229). ½ mile (800 metres) north-east of Buxton church on the B1354 Aylsham to Coltishall road.
Open daily.

A coping stone on this attractive weatherboarded mill bears the date 1754 although it was mainly built in the nineteenth century. There has been a watermill here since pre-Conquest times, and it was one of the last working watermills in Norfolk. There is now a restaurant at the mill and furnishing and interior design shops. Boating is available on the river.

Caston Windmill (OS 144: TL 951982). Telephone: 095383 551. 3 miles (5 km) south-east of Watton on A1075, turning left on to the B1077.
Open by appointment.

Caston Mill was built in 1864 and last worked in 1940. It is owned by the millwright John Lawn, who is restoring it. The six-storey

tower is tarred and the cap is boat-shaped.

Clayrack Drainage Mill. See How Hill, page 121.

Cley Windmill (OS 133: TG 045441). Telephone: 0263 740209. In the centre of the village on A149.
Open Easter to September.

This well-known and much photographed landmark stands overlooking the marshes. It is a brick tower mill and last worked in 1912. It has been converted to a guest-house and is open to the public in summer.

Denver Windmill (OS 143: TF 605013). Telephone: 0366 2285. NMPT. ½ mile (800 metres) from Denver church along Sluice Road.
Open April to September, on Wednesdays, Saturdays and bank holidays.

Most of the machinery of this fine six-storey tower mill is intact and new sails and a working fantail have been added. It was built in 1835 and has a distinctive onion-shaped cap. There is a former steam mill, granary and engine shed attached. Extensive repairs on this windmill have now been completed.

Dereham Windmill, Cherry Lane, Norwich Road, Dereham. Telephone (group bookings

only): 0362 694725.
Open in summer, Thursdays, Fridays and Saturdays in the early afternoon and until late afternoon on Sundays.

The cap, fantail and sails of this brick tower mill built in 1836 have been restored by the owners and part of the mill machinery can be seen but the mill is not in working order.

Foulden Watermill (OS 143: TL 748991). 1 mile (1.6 km) north of Northwold.
Not open to the public.

The mill is not a spectacular building but it is historically interesting as there has been a watermill on this site since Domesday. Guided tours are available and there are facilities for fishing and camping.

Garboldisham Windmill (OS 144: TM 003805). Telephone: 095381 593. ¹/₂ mile (800 metres) south of the village, which is on the A1066 Thetford to Diss road.
Open Wednesday and Friday mornings throughout the year.

This post mill is one of only two to survive more or less intact in Norfolk. The round-house has been restored and the three-storey timber buck is under restoration. The mill produces organic flour using modern milling equipment. It is privately owned and sometimes open to the public.

Great Bircham Windmill (OS 132: TF 760327). Telephone: 048523 393. On high ground to the west of the village, near Docking.
Open daily April to September. Tea room closed on Saturdays.

The sails of this beautiful tower mill turn on windy days and from a gallery on the stone floor there are excellent views over the countryside. The mill, which has an ogee-shaped top, is being restored by the owners. There is a display of baking equipment. Guided tours are given, and there is a play area for children under seven.

Gunton Sawmill. See page 116.

Hobbs Windpump, Horning (OS 134: TG 347162). NMPT. On the east bank of the river Bure.

Garboldisham Windmill.

Letheringsett Watermill.

Narborough Watermill.

Open by arrangement with the Norfolk Mills and Pumps Trust or enquire at Wild's Boatyard nearby.

This interesting open-framed timber-trestle windpump is being restored.

Horsey Windpump (OS 134: TG 457221). National Trust. Telephone: NT Regional Office, 0263 733471. 2¹/₂ miles (4 km) northeast of Potter Heigham on B1159.

Open during daylight from April to September.

There are good views across the marshes from this four-storey windpump, which was acquired by the National Trust in 1948 and has been restored.

How Hill, Ludham.

At How Hill (see page 67) are Boardman's Mill, an open-trestle type mill owned by the Norfolk Mills and Pumps Trust (OS 134: TG 370192) and Turf Fen Windpump, also NMPT (TG 369188). Ranworth Hollow Post Mill (TG 368195) has also been relocated at How Hill and is known as Clayrack Windpump. All three drainage mills are visible at all times from the river and public footpaths.

Letheringsett Watermill (OS 133: TG 063388). Telephone: 0263 713153. ¹/₂ mile (800 metres) south of the Holt to King's Lynn road (A148).

Open all year daily, but mornings only on Saturdays and on Sunday afternoons only in the summer.

The millstones are turning again at this small mill, built in the Tuscan style in 1757 to serve the Letheringsett Hall estate. It has been restored on the initiative of an estate worker and now produces wholemeal stoneground flour. The mill sells flour and other products.

Little Cressingham Wind and Water Mill (OS 144: TF 869002). NMPT. 2 miles (3 km) west of Watton off B1108.

Open on second Sunday of each month from May to October and all Sundays in August.

This attractive old mill with its miller's house on the river Wissey is unique in Norfolk in being a combined wind and water mill. Two pairs of stones on the first floor are designed to be driven by the waterwheel and two on the third floor by wind power. The mill is being restored.

Loddon Watermill (OS 134: TM 362990). Telephone: 0508 28146. Between Loddon and Chedgrave.

This 400-year-old watermill is considered to be the oldest in East Anglia and the only all-timber mill in England. The machinery is a working replica of the original and the owners have set up a museum, art gallery, antique shop and restaurant in the mill.

Stoke Holy Cross Watermill.

Narborough Watermill, Narborough, King's Lynn PE32 1TE (OS 132: TF 747132). Telephone: 0670 338005.

The Nar was once navigable as far as Narborough, as the Ship Inn testifies, and there were two watermills and a malting, but one of the mills and the malting are now derelict. The other mill, a handsome brick building, was built in 1845 but by 1900 it was in a bad state of repair. The mill still has its milling machinery.

Old Buckenham Cornmill, Old Buckenham (OS 134: TM 062909).

This corn mill has the largest-diameter tower in England. It can be viewed externally from a car-park site. The mill is to reopen in 1995 following extensive repairs.

St Benet's Abbey Mill (OS 134: TG 380158). On the confluence of the rivers Bure and Ant. *Open all year.*

The ruins of this eighteenth-century mill built into remains of a gateway of St Benet's Abbey (see page 81) are well-known as a subject for photographers and artists, including J. S. Cotman. It was once used to crush colza seeds to produce oil for lamps. It can be reached by boat or along a by-road from Ludham.

St Olaves Windpump (OS 134: TM 457997). NMPT. For further information contact the Bridge Stores: telephone 0493 488230. On the east bank of the Waveney, just below St Olaves Bridge on A143.
Open all year; keys are available from the Bridge Stores.

St Olaves tiny boarded timber-trestle windpump has been restored by the Norfolk Mills and Pumps Trust with grants from the Broads Authority. It can be reached by footpath from the bridge. This windpump is also known as Priory Mill.

Snettisham Watermill, Station Road, Snettisham PE31 7QJ. Telephone: 0485 42180.

This mill was built in 1800 of local carrstone and pantiles and the original machinery survives. In 1986 it was brought back into production and is open to visitors. There are demonstrations, an exhibition, gardens with a waterfall and ducks on the millpond. A plaque at the mill explains that it was 'erected at a time of scarcity by voluntary subscription for the common benefit of the neighbourhood'.

Starston Windpump (OS 156: TM 232843). Owner: R. Lomb-Taylor, Conifer Hill, Starston IP20 9NP. Telephone: 0379 852394. 1 mile (1.6 km) from Harleston off B1134. *Open daily. The key is available from the owner.*

This very attractive hollow-post windpump with a brick roundhouse was once used to supply water to a neighbouring farm. It has been restored and the sails, which have canvas not wooden slats, now turn.

Stoke Holy Cross Watermill (Old Mill Restaurant) (OS 134: TG 232019). Telephone: 05086 3337.

Jeremiah Colman leased this mill and began making the now famous mustard in 1814. The enterprise grew and soon it was the centre of a large factory complex. In 1862 the factory moved to Norwich and the mill is now a restaurant.

Stow High Windmill, Paston (OS 133: TG 316358.) Telephone: Paston Mill Cottage, 0263 720298. ¹/2 mile (800 metres) south of Mundesley on B1159.
Open daily.

This spectacular mill was built in about 1827 and was working until 1930. It has been partially restored and the fantail is operating. It is privately owned but is cared for by the Norfolk Mills and Pumps Trust. It is open in summer and there are guided tours.

Stracey Arms Windpump, Acle (OS 134; TG 442090). NMPT. Near Stracey Arms public house, on A47 Acle New Road.
Open daily April to September.

This windpump, a four-storey brick tower 'mill', stands on the banks of the river Bure. It is said to be built on a raft of pitch pine set on 40 foot (12 metre) piles driven into the marsh. It has been restored to full working order.

Sutton Windmill, Sutton, Norwich NR12 9RZ (OS 134: TG 396239). Telephone: 0692 581195. ¹/2 mile (800 metres) east of Sutton.
Open daily Easter to September.

Sutton corn mill is thought to be the tallest surviving windmill in Britain. It has nine floors and is being restored by its owners. The mill is painted in its original bright colours, red and blue, probably chosen for patriotic reasons. There is a museum of bygones and the mill is open throughout the summer.

Thrigby Corn Mill, Mill Cottage, Thrigby NR29 3DY (OS 134: TG 468121). Telephone: 0493 369596.
Open daily – ask at Mill Cottage.

The owners of this post mill, one of only two in Norfolk, are restoring it and hope to grind corn again one day. The mill was built in 1790 and last milled corn in 1890; the top of the mill was then removed, leaving only the roundhouse. The mill can be viewed by arrangement with the owners.

Thurne Dyke Windpump (OS 134: TG 401159). NMPT. 3 miles (5 km) north of Acle.
'Jack' is open every Sunday afternoon, May to September.

This white-painted windpump is one of the most distinctive of the Broadland windmills, having been 'raised', hence its unusual shape. It is known locally as 'Jack'. The sister mill, 'Jenny', is across the water. The windpump

Thurne Dyke Windpump.

has been restored. 'Jenny' or St Benet's Windpump (TG 399156) has also been restored. When the wind is strong, the two windpumps can sometimes be seen turning together, but 'Jenny' is not open to the public.

Turf Fen Windpump. See How Hill, page 121.

Wicklewood Windmill (OS 144: TG 077028). NMPT. For information telephone Mr Woodrow: 0953 603694. 2½ miles (4 km) west of Wymondham on B1135.
Open from May to September on the third Sunday of the month in the afternoon.

Wicklewood corn mill was built in 1845 and last worked in 1942. The brick tower has five storeys and a boat-shaped top. It has been restored by the Norfolk Mills and Pumps Trust and the tower repainted with black waterproof paint (formerly coal tar was used). There is a small exhibition.

Wicklewood Windmill.

Mill Farm Rare Breeds, Hindringham.

12
Other places to visit

Alby Craft Centre, Cromer Road, Alby, Erpingham, Norwich NR11 7QE. Telephone: 0263 761590. On A140.
Open daily except Mondays and Saturdays, Easter to September.

Gallery studio workshops, a showroom for locally made furniture, a honeypot shop, a lace museum and a buttery and craft gift shop are among the attractions of this craft centre set up in restored brick and flint farm buildings. The George Dennis collection of about three thousand bottles is on display – the only bottle museum display in Britain.

Banham Zoo and Monkey Sanctuary, The Grove, Banham, Norwich NR16 2HE. Telephone: 095387 771.
Open daily.

The zoo park is a sanctuary for many rare animals from around the world, including ruffed lemurs, maned wolves, zebras, camels and snow leopards. Other attractions include a putting green and pets' corner.

Buxton Mill Craft Centre, Buxton. Telephone: 060546 410.

This watermill on the river Bure (see page 119) makes an attractive setting for studios selling a variety of crafts from pottery to carpets. There are also ducks and swans to be fed and boating on the river.

The Bygone Village, Fleggburgh, Great Yarmouth NR29 3AF. Telephone: 0493 369770.
Open throughout the year, Sunday to Thursday, and every day in the summer season.

The Bygone Village is set in over 30 acres (12 hectares) of woodland. Visitors can explore craft cottages and workshops, the village inn and the working sawmill and stone quarry. They can ride the narrow-gauge railway and the fairground 'gallopers'. Live shows throughout the day include the wonderful Compton-Christie cinema organ. A

new attraction is 'Myths and Legends of East Anglia', set in the cellars of the new hall.

Caithness Crystal, Oldmeadow Road, Hardwick Industrial Estate, King's Lynn PE30 4JT. Telephone: 0553 765111.
Open daily June to mid September. Factory tours Mondays to Fridays. Shop open throughout year.

This glass factory invites visitors to watch glassmaking and glass engraving at close quarters and to see glassmaking tools and moulds. An introductory talk is provided, and locally made glass is on sale.

Cockley Cley Iceni Village and Museums, Cockley Cley, Swaffham PE37 8AG. Telephone: 0760 721339.
Open daily April to September.

This reconstruction of an Iceni settlement of the first century AD gives an insight into the way of life of early inhabitants of Norfolk. The site is believed to be that of an actual village of the time of Queen Boudicca (Boadicea). A fifteenth-century cottage and forge house a museum depicting East Anglian life in that period and earlier. There is a museum of carriages, vintage engines and farm implements and a nature trail, and close by is a Saxon church of about AD 630.

Congham Hall Herb Garden, Conningham Hall, Grimston, King's Lynn PE32 1AH. Telephone: 0485 600250.
Open daily, except Saturdays, from April to October in the afternoon.

More than two hundred different herbs, as well as interesting vegetables, are grown in this garden attached to a hotel. It is based on a seventeenth-century design. Tours of the garden, including a lunch based on home-grown vegetables, may be booked.

Courtyard Farm, Ringstead, Hunstanton PE36 5LQ. Telephone: 048525 369.

Open throughout the year.

There are farm walks through beautiful countryside to enjoy on this 750 acre (300 hectare) mixed farm near the north Norfolk coast. The farm is managed by a trust as a profit-making enterprise but with conservation of the countryside also a priority. Basic accommodation is available overnight at Bunkhouse Barn: booking is advisable.

Cranes Watering Farm, Starston, near Harleston. Telephone: 0397 852387.
Open daily, Tuesdays to Saturdays, except in January and on bank holiday and Sunday mornings.

This working farm with pigs, sheep and cows is open to farm-shop customers. A visit is very much a hands-on experience and wellingtons are required!

The Curiosity Street Experience, Reepham Station, Station Road, Reepham, Norfolk NR10 4LJ. Telephone: 0603 871187.
Open daily April to October. Telephone for winter opening times.

Thousands of exhibits relating to the household products and advertising of the past bring to life a bygone age of shopping. They are housed in a former country railway station, and there is a display on the station's history. Other attractions include giant outdoor games, and bicycles may be hired for exploring Marriott's Way (see page 58) and nearby country lanes.

Dinosaur Park, Weston Estate, Weston Longville, Norwich NR9 5JW. Telephone: 0603 870245.
Open daily April to October.

Life-size models of dinosaurs are set among 300 acres (120 hectares) of woodland, offering wonderful photographic opportunities. Other attractions include a maze, an adventure playground and a Bygones Museum.

East Anglian Falconry Centre, Goat Inn, Skeyton NR10 5DH. Telephone: 0692 69600.
Open daily in summer and Tuesday to Sunday in winter.

There are over two hundred birds of prey at this centre including the rare goshawk,

peregrine falcon, harris and redtail hawks and eagle and snowy owls. Some of the birds have been sent to Skeyton after being injured in the wild. There are flying displays and conducted tours.

Elmham Park Vineyards and Winery, Elmham House, North Elmham, East Dereham NR20 5JY. Telephone: 0362 668571.
Conducted tours by appointment.

The vineyards are situated in Elmham Park and one may be seen just across the road from the Anglo-Saxon cathedral. Tours, wine tasting and a slide show are available for groups on summer evenings.

Equine Rest and Rehabilitation Centres at Overa House Farm, Larling, near Thetford (telephone: 0953 717114) and at Anne Colvin House, Snetterton, near Attleborough (telephone: 0953 498682).
Open Wednesdays and Sunday afternoons, except on 25th and 26th December, and by appointment.

At both these centres, which are within 2 miles (3 km) of each other, horses, donkeys and ponies are being cared for by the International League for the Protection of Horses. They may be seen in their paddocks and stables.

Kingdom of the Sea, Marine Parade, Great Yarmouth, Norfolk NR30 3AH. Telephone: 0493 330631.
Open daily.

Walking through the underwater tunnel, the visitor comes face to face with tropical sharks and other forms of marine life. There are more than 25 marine dioramas on display: subjects include Breydon Water and Wiveton Dunes.

Kingdom of the Sea, Southern Promenade, Hunstanton PE36 5BH. Telephone: 0485 533576.
Open daily.

A special marine tunnel enables visitors to walk through the water and view marine life at close quarters, including seals recovering after being treated for infections. Later the seals are returned to the open sea.

Langham Glass, The Long Barn, North Street, Langham, Holt NR25 7DG. Telephone: 0328 830511.

Open Mondays to Fridays throughout the year, also on Saturdays, Sundays and bank holidays from May to October.

The traditional glassmaking can be seen in a converted eighteenth-century barn in this pretty village near Blakeney.

Mill Farm Rare Breeds, Hindringham, Norfolk NR21 0PR. Telephone: 0328 878560.

Open daily Tuesday to Sunday, Easter to October, and bank holidays.

Here can be seen examples of breeds of animal that were once common on English farms but now are rarely found, such as Shire horses and Norfolk black turkeys. Children have an opportunity to meet lambs, goats and rabbits in the pets' corner and in the wildlife area there are owl boxes, a pond and English flower meadows. In season there are demonstrations of heavy horses at work, sheep shearing and spinning.

Natural Surroundings, Bayfield Estate, Holt NR25 7JN. Telephone: 0263 711091.

Open daily Easter to October, Thursdays to Sundays for the rest of the year.

Wildlife and organic gardening are demonstrated on this attractive 8 acre (3.2 hectare) estate near Glandford. There are also 'natural' cornfields, orchid meadows, woodland walks, a herb garden, wild flower centre and a nature trail.

Norfolk Lavender, Caley Mill, Heacham, King's Lynn PE31 7JE. Telephone: 0485 70384.

Open daily except for two weeks over Christmas.

This is England's only lavender farm, on the riverside, with gardens of lavender, herbs and roses. There is a large countryside gift shop and a lavender and herb shop. Informative tours are given, and this is the home of the National Collection of Lavender.

Norfolk Rare Breeds Centre, Decoy Farm, Ormesby St Michael, Great Yarmouth NR29 3LY. Telephone: 0493 732990.

Open daily except Saturdays from April to mid September and on Sundays in winter.

Rare breeds of cattle, sheep, pigs and poultry may be seen on the farm, as well as donkeys, goats, heavy horses, rabbits and waterfowl. There is a small farm museum and crafts

A European lynx with her cubs at the Norfolk Wildlife Park at Great Witchingham.

are on sale.

Norfolk Shire Horse Centre, West Runton Stables, West Runton, Cromer NR27 9QH. Telephone: 026375 339.
Open Easter to October, Sundays to Fridays and bank holiday Saturdays.

There are draught horses, native mountain and moorland ponies, some with foals, and a collection of young farm animals at this centre celebrating working horses. Visitors can watch harnessing and working demonstrations and ride in farm carts. There are also wagons, carts, gypsy caravans and bygones on display, a riding school and a picnic area.

Norfolk Wildlife Park and Play Centre, Great Witchingham, Norwich NR9 5QS. Telephone: 0603 872274.
Open daily April to October.

This park has one of the largest collections of European birds and mammals in the world. They are exhibited under natural conditions in large enclosures. They include European bison, wild pig, otter, seal, six species of deer and Barbary apes. The park also has areas for children, a pets' corner, rides on a sleigh pulled by a team of reindeer, and a woodland steam railway.

Otter Trust, Earsham, Bungay, Suffolk NR35 2AF. Telephone: 0986 893470.
Open daily April to October.

The otter sanctuary has been established on the Norfolk side of the river Waveney, and there are three lakes and a stream in the otter breeding enclosure. Otters are bred here and reintroduced into the wild. There are also riverside walks, a deer wood and an exhibition on the work of the Otter Trust and on the conservation of wetlands. As well as otters, many different species of waterfowl are to be seen on the lakes.

Park Farm, Snettisham, King's Lynn PE31 7NQ. Telephone: 0485 542425.
Open daily mid March to mid October.

This commercial farm offers visitors a real farm experience. There are cattle, sheep, goats, free-range chickens and red deer to be seen, guided tours on a tractor and trailer or in a safari Land-Rover, trails to follow and a visitor centre.

Pensthorpe Waterfowl Trust, Pensthorpe, Fakenham NR21 0LN. Telephone: 0328 851465.
Open daily April to December and on Saturdays and Sundays January to March.

A vineyard at Pulham Market.

More than 120 species of waterfowl have been introduced to this man-made nature park, centred on lakes formed in disused gravel pits. Around the lakes there are paths through meadows, marshes and woodland rich in wild flowers, including orchids. Many species of marshland birds, butterflies and dragonflies may be seen and in winter migratory waterfowl visit the lakes. There is an information centre and an adventure playground. The site is fully accessible for disabled visitors.

Pettitts Animal Adventure Park, Camp Hill, Reedham NR13 3UA. Telephone: 0493 700094.
Open daily except Saturdays mid April to October.

A Falabella miniature horse stud, donkey rides, tame animals and birds to feed, rides on a narrow-gauge railway and feathercraft and taxidermy displays are among the attractions at these gardens founded in 1921. There are children's shows, with live entertainment and costume animal characters.

Pulham Market Vineyard, Mill Lane, Pulham Market, Diss IP21 4XL. Telephone: 0379 676672.
Open by appointment May to October.

Magdalen wines from this vineyard, planted in 1972 from Moselle vine stocks, have won prizes against wines from all over the world. Visitors are welcome to walk round and taste the wines.

Redwings Horse Sanctuary, Hill Top Farm, Hall Lane, Frettenham, Norwich NR12 7LT. Telephone: 0603 737432.
Open in the afternoons on Sundays from Easter to mid December and on Mondays in July and August.

More than three hundred horses, ponies and donkeys are being cared for at this sanctuary, where neglected children's ponies, retired beach donkeys and horses that have been ill treated are given a kind and permanent home. There are pony rides and a farm walk.

Textile Centre, Hindringham Road, Great Walsingham NR22 6DR. Telephone: 0328 820009.
Open daily March to mid November.

Screen printing on textiles is demonstrated by Sheila Rowse and her assistants. The hand-printed designs produced in the workshop on household linens and clothing are on sale in the craft shop.

Thrigby Hall Wildlife Gardens, Filby, Great Yarmouth NR29 3DR. Telephone: 0493 369477.
Open daily.

The animals at this zoo are from Asia and they include snow leopards, Sumatran tigers, antelope, gibbons, crocodiles and many exotic birds. In the landscaped grounds of the fine hall are picnic areas and adventure play areas.

Tudor Tour. Information from tourist information centres (see page 141). A leaflet is available.

This 60 mile (100 km) signposted circular route takes about a day to complete by car. It includes many out-of-the-way villages with buildings dating back to the sixteenth century. The tour leaves Norwich on the A1067 and includes Attlebridge, Alderford and Swannington in the Wensum valley, then goes to Haveringland, Marsham and Blickling in the Bure valley. The route then winds through villages around Salle, then on to Lenwade and the Ringland Hills and back to Norwich.

Willow Farm Flowers, Cangate, Neatishead, Norwich NR12 8YH. Telephone: 0603 783588.
Open daily (shorter hours on Sundays).

Watch dried flowers being arranged and walk round the flower field during the growing season. The shop sells bunches and arrangements of dried flowers.

Wroxham Barns, Tunstead Road, Hoveton, Norwich NR12 8QU. Telephone: 0603 783762.
Open daily.

A collection of restored eighteenth-century barns houses craft workshops and a craft gallery, set in 7 acres (2.8 hectares) of parkland with a picnic and playground area. There is also a 'Junior Farm' to explore. Dogs are not allowed.

13
Famous people

The reputation that Norfolk people have of 'doing different' has perhaps given them a will to achieve; certainly Norfolk has plenty of famous sons and daughters and proudly celebrates them with monuments, pub dedications, special exhibitions and wall plaques. Some are nationally or even internationally famous, for example Lord Nelson, Sir Robert Walpole, Thomas Paine, J. S. Cotman and Elizabeth Fry.

Agricultural reformers

It is not surprising that one of England's foremost farming counties should have produced agricultural reformers. **Charles, second Viscount Townshend** (1674-1738), known as 'Turnip' Townshend, is famous for popularising the Norfolk four-course rotation, alternating root crops, such as turnips, and grass with corn, and improving light soils by 'marling', or spreading on the fields a mixture of clay and lime dug from pits. Marl pits are still a feature of the Norfolk landscape. Charles Townshend grew up at Raynham Hall, one of the finest of Norfolk's seven-

teenth-century houses, which his father had built. The house, which is not open to the public, is still owned by the Townshend family. His father died while Charles was still a boy and he inherited the estate at the age of thirteen. Trustees arranged his education, which was completed by a Grand Tour of Europe. He then spent more than twenty years in public service as ambassador to Holland and later directing Britain's foreign policy. While in Holland he became interested in Dutch agricultural methods and the growing of turnips. As a result, when Townshend finally retired to Raynham in 1730 many of the improvements he introduced on the estate had their origins in methods practised in Holland. He enclosed fields and planted hedges, improved fertility and adopted the new cropping systems. His ideas were taken up by his neighbours and Norfolk became a wealthy exporter of grain through ports like King's Lynn.

The Coke family (later Earls of Leicester) of Holkham Hall (see page 100) were near neighbours of the Townshends. **Thomas**

The monument to Edward Coke, Chief Justice of England, at Tittleshall church.

William Coke (1752-1842), popularly known as 'Coke of Norfolk', was another agricultural reformer and like Townshend also in public service. Most of the great landlords were happy to leave the farming of their estates to tenant farmers while they pursued the lives of country gentlemen. Coke, however, involved himself in farming and transformed his land from sheep pastures where 'two sheep fought over a blade of grass' to productive mixed farms. He instituted an annual sheepshearing festival which enabled farmers to exchange ideas and learn new techniques. He was created first Earl of Leicester (of the second creation) in recognition of his services to agriculture. When he died a monument to him was erected by his tenants and stands in the grounds of Holkham Hall. Several monuments to his ancestors can be found in Tittleshall church, south of Fakenham.

Politics and revolution

The greatest of Norfolk's many squire politicians was **Sir Robert Walpole** (1676-1745). Two paintings of Sir Robert, Britain's first prime minister, hang at his home at Houghton Hall (see page 101). One shows him with his hunting dogs on his estate as the Norfolk squire and the other shows him in his Garter robes, every inch the great politician. Another portrait of Sir Robert in his Garter robes hangs over the mantelpiece at Number 10 Downing Street in London. Sir Robert was a very forceful, pleasure-loving character, not without his coarse side, but above all he was an astute financier and politician. He served as prime minister for 21 years and brought peace and prosperity to Britain. In addition he had a passion for art and architecture and assembled a brilliant collection of paintings at Houghton, which his grandson sold to Catharine the Great of Russia. The collection now hangs in the Hermitage Collection in St Petersburg.

During the last years of Sir Robert Walpole's time as prime minister, one of the most remarkable political writers and radical thinkers of the eighteenth century was growing up in Thetford. **Thomas Paine** (1737-1809) was the son of a Quaker and it was from the Quakers that the young Thomas first acquired

The statue of Thomas Paine at Thetford.

his humanitarian ideas. He was well educated at the free grammar school at Thetford and when he left school he went to London, first following his father's trade as a corsetmaker but later becoming a customs officer. In London he also pursued his interest in politics and philosophy and wrote his first pamphlet – on better salaries for customs officers, which cost him his job. An American politician persuaded him to go to America and there he became editor of a magazine and began writing in earnest on political topics. In 1787 he sailed for France, where the revolutionary ideas which led to the French Revolution were gaining ground, and then on to England. He began work on his most famous book, *The Rights of Man* (1791), which was at once condemned as seditious in England. He left hurriedly for France, where the French Revolution was now underway, and was given a hero's welcome. A year later he was arrested, perhaps because he was under criticism in America and one faction of the French revolutionaries was anxious to placate the United States. In the confused situation of the time he was lucky to escape the guillotine.

Finally he was released and returned to America to continue his political writing. After his death in 1819 his bones were brought back to England but no one knows where they were buried. A statue to Paine (see page 51), paid for by subscriptions raised in the USA, stands in Thetford. His house (now part of a hotel) has a commemorative plaque and the Ancient House Museum (see page 112) has a permanent exhibition devoted to his life and work.

Sir George Edwards (1850-1933) was another Norfolk man who campaigned for the rights of man. After campaigning for years to improve the working and living conditions of agricultural workers, he founded the National Union of Land Workers (later the National Union of Farm Workers) in 1906. He was born at Marsham in north Norfolk, the son of a discharged soldier who worked, when work was available, as a labourer on the land and sometimes as a bricklayer. George's mother was a hand-loom weaver, working at home on piece work, sometimes for sixteen hours a day. The Edwardses could not afford schooling for their children and George began work at the age of six as a crow-scarer. At sixteen he entered into farm service. He later married and his wife taught him to read. By 1893 he was secretary of the Norfolk Labourers' Union. In 1906 he was elected to the Norfolk County Council. In 1918 he was made an alderman and in 1919 he was awarded the OBE. He served as Labour member of Parliament for South Norfolk from 1920 to 1922 and from 1923 to 1924 and in 1930 he was knighted. All his life he was a staunch Methodist and for many years he was a lay preacher. He continued working for the rights of agricultural workers until just before his death at the age of 83.

An earlier radical Norfolk hero, **Robert Kett** (1492-1549), of Wymondham, and his brother William were executed for their part in an uprising in 1549. There was widespread unrest at this time as a result of the dissolution of the monasteries by Henry VIII and the appropriation of church land by the wealthy. In addition commons were being enclosed and peasant farmers deprived of pasturage. At Wymondham there was great resentment at the greed of a local landowner, Sir John Flowerdew, who had appropriated land and materials from the abbey buildings. Kett's rebellion began as a celebration of the arrest and imprisonment of the third Duke of Norfolk as a result of intrigues in the court of Henry VIII. The Duke was a notoriously repressive feudal landowner. Robert Kett was also a minor landowner but he took up the cause of the peasantry and lesser landowners and in a short time it is claimed that he had a following of 12,000. He marched on Norwich, one of the wealthiest cities in England, pausing at 'Kett's Oak' at Hethersett, which can still be seen. At first the city authorities attempted to reason with the rebels but Kett's men were intent on furthering their cause and perhaps on plundering the city. Troops were sent from London but Kett defeated them and their commander, Lord Sheffield, was killed. The Earl of Warwick was sent with reinforcements and Kett's army was defeated on St Martin's Plain. Robert Kett was captured and hanged from the castle battlements, his brother in Wymondham. Some of the soldiers are buried in the churchyards of St Martin at Palace and St Jude's Tombland. Robert Kett is celebrated as a defender of the rights of ordinary people in Norfolk. Most of what he and his followers fought for – a juster system of land tenure and church reforms – was granted within a generation.

Heroes of the sea

The sea is never far away in Norfolk and it is therefore not surprising that one of England's greatest naval heroes, **Horatio, Lord Nelson** (1758-1805), was, in his words, 'a Norfolk man and I glory in being so'. In 1805 Napoleon's dream of sending an army across the Channel to conquer England were shattered by the naval tactics of a son of a Norfolk vicar. Horatio Nelson was born at Burnham Thorpe in a house that no longer stands. He had a strict upbringing and was educated at the Norwich Grammar School (where he is commemorated by a statue in the forecourt) and at the Paston School, North Walsham. At eleven he went to sea in a merchantman under his uncle, Maurice Suckling. By the time he was 21 he was a captain in the navy but in

1787 he was suspended on half pay after disputes with senior officers and came back with his wife and family to Burnham Thorpe. In 1793 he was back at sea on active service. The Spanish admiral's sword that he acquired at the battle of St Vincent was later presented to the City of Norwich and may be seen at the Guildhall and a portrait of Nelson is in Blackfriars' Hall. He visited Great Yarmouth three times. On one occasion after the battle of the Nile he was given the Freedom of the Borough and on a visit in 1801 his portrait was painted and now hangs in the Town Hall. Nelson was a brilliant naval tactician and his defeat of the French and Spanish navies at Trafalgar near Cadiz in 1805 changed the course of history and prevented Napoleon from invading England. The battle, however, cost Nelson his life. He had asked to be buried in Norfolk but so great was the nation's admiration for him that he was given a state funeral and buried in St Paul's Cathedral in London. Hangings from the funeral carriage, which was shaped fore and aft like his flagship the *Victory,* are preserved in the Maritime Museum at Lowestoft. In 1819 the 144 foot (44 metre) high Nelson Monument was erected at Great Yarmouth. One of Nelson's seamen, James Sharman, a Yarmouth man, was appointed caretaker of the monument. Dickens is reputed to have visited Sharman and to have based the character of Ham Peggotty in *David Copperfield* on him. The memory of Nelson lives on in Norfolk; even today there are no less than fourteen Nelson, Lord Nelson or Hero pubs in the county.

Captain George Vancouver (1757-98) was born just a year after Nelson in New Conduit Street, King's Lynn, where a plaque marks the spot, although the house has been demolished. His father was a customs officer, a lucrative post in those days, at the Old Custom House (see page 30). King's Lynn was a busy port and the young Vancouver would have been familiar with the trading ships from around the world that called at Lynn. At fourteen he went to sea, sailing with Captain James Cook to the South Seas, and in 1766 he sailed on Cook's ill-fated voyage on the *Discovery*. When Cook was killed in Ha-

The Old Custom House at King's Lynn, where George Vancouver's father was a customs officer.

waii, Vancouver played an heroic part in re-covering the body. Later Vancouver com-manded ships on voyages of discovery to Australia and Canada where, as a result of his diplomacy, the island of Vancouver was ceded to Britain. In 1797 he retired from the navy in poor health and died in 1798. A number of British Columbian place-names, among them Snettisham, Lynn and Holkham, are a re-minder of the Norfolk connection.

Captain Henry Blogg (1876-1954), the Cromer lifeboatman,was of humbler birth but no less courageous. The Norfolk coast off Cromer with its shifting sandbanks has many hazards for ships and the Cromer lifeboat was constantly being called out. Henry Blogg served in the Cromer lifeboats for 53 years, 38 of them as coxswain. He took part in no less than 387 call-outs and saved 873 lives. No other lifeboatman ever won so many gal-lantry awards, which included three gold med-als and the George Cross. Henry Blogg was a big man in every way – genial and modest as well as courageous. He was often to be seen on the beach preparing for a fishing trip in his oilies smelling of fish and tar or in a 'slop' or in a garnsey knitted by his wife Ann or around the town in a reefer jacket. His medals, which in his lifetime were always tucked away in a drawer, are on display at the Old Boathouse Lifeboat Museum (see page 104). The Cromer Museum has a reconstruction of a fisherman's cottage very like Captain Blogg's simple home. When he died his coffin was decorated to resemble a lifeboat with a wreath in the shape of a ship's wheel.

Social reformers

Norfolk produced many social reformers and philanthropists during the eighteenth and nineteenth centuries, many of them associ-ated with the nonconformist communities in Norwich, in particular the Society of Friends (Quakers). The banking family of J. J. Gurney of Earlham Hall and later the Colman family, whose fortune was founded on their mustard mill, were among the most prominent.

Famous women reformers and writers

Many Norfolk women were active in social reform, the most famous among them being **Elizabeth Fry** (1780-1845), a member of the Gurney family. She was born at Earlham Hall, now part of the University of East Anglia. She was impressed by American Quakers and adopted the distinctive Quaker dress and manner of speech, to her family's dismay. Later she married a fellow Quaker, Joseph Fry, and had nine children. She started visiting prisons in 1816 and became commit-ted to improving conditions, particularly for the women, and was a firm believer in re-habilitation. She was an assiduous diarist – 44 volumes of her diaries are kept in Norwich at the Friends Meeting House (see page 90). The eighteenth-century Gurney Court, Nor-wich, was once the Gurney family's town house.

Amelia Opie (1769-1853) was born in Nor-wich and is best-known as a novelist and poet. She married John Opie of London but returned to live in what is now known as Opie Street in Norwich. In later life she gave up her literary and musical interests, became a Quaker and joined the anti-slavery movement. She also helped Elizabeth Fry with her phil-anthropic work.

Harriet Martineau (1802-76) was also in-volved with the anti-slavery movement. She was born in Norwich, the daughter of a cloth manufacturer. Harriet was a nervous and sickly child, afflicted with deafness, which later worsened. The family business collapsed when she was a young woman and she re-mained single. She turned to writing and con-tributed to many of the more serious journals of the day, writing stories and also articles on religion and morals. She was an early femi-nist, believing strongly in the need to educate women, and was the first woman journalist to work on a national newspaper.

Fanny Burney (1752-1840) of King's Lynn belongs to the same period and is ad-mired as a diarist and novelist, particularly for her novel *Evelina* (1778), but she was of a less serious nature and more romantically in-clined.

Literary figures

There is no shortage of famous literary fig-ures in Norfolk. The earliest was a woman, better known as a religious mystic, **Mother Julian** (1342-*c*.1429), but she is considered to be the first English woman of letters. Her *Revelations of Divine Love* describe her mystical experiences while living as an anchoress in a small hermitage in the churchyard of St Julian's in Norwich (see page 90). She lived to a great age. Her reputation as a religious mystic has grown in modern times and the Julian Centre, church and shrine off Rouen Road in Norwich are open daily.

The life of **Margery Kempe** (1373 to *c*.1440), the celebrated mystic and pilgrim of King's Lynn, was written by an unknown cleric (or clerics) shortly after her death and is described as the first biography in English. Margery Kempe was born in King's Lynn, the daughter of a prominent citizen, married in 1393 and for fifteen years lived a worldly life. She then became committed to a life of celibacy, prayer and mysticism. She undertook pilgrimages to the Holy Land, Rome, Compostella in Spain and eastern Europe. Her eccentric beliefs and way of life were often questioned but she had many powerful supporters.

The giant among Norfolk's illustrious literary figures is **Sir Thomas Browne** (1605-82), whose statue stands on Hay Hill near Norwich Market. He was the son of a Norwich silk merchant and studied medicine at Oxford, Montpellier and Padua before returning to Norwich to practise as a physician. There he married and had twelve children. He lived in an undistinguished house in Orford Place; his ornate timber mantelpiece is on display at Norwich Castle Museum. He was a scholar as well as a respected physician and wrote on medicine, archaeology, philosophy and natural history in a distinctive baroque style which is much admired for its rich imagery. His most famous book was *Religio Medici* (1643) and his description of iron-age urns unearthed in west Norfolk in *Urn Burial* is a classic of its kind. He is buried at St Peter Mancroft church in Norwich and his death mask, a fine oil painting and the household book of the Harbord family containing seven of his herb-based prescriptions are also kept there. In his writings, Sir Thomas does not comment on the issues raised by the Civil War then raging but he refused to contribute funds to the parliamentary army, a brave stand to make in anti-royalist Norwich. For this he was knighted by Charles II in St Andrew's Hall in 1671.

The poet **John Skelton** (1460-1529) was born at Diss, where he later became rector. He was tutor to Henry VIII and his poems are often political and satirical.

William Cowper (1733-1800), the poet and writer of the hymn 'God moves in a mysterious way...', lived in East Dereham from 1795 until his death. He is buried in St Thomas's chapel and is also commemorated by a Victorian stained glass window by Flaxman in St Nicholas's church, East Dereham. There is a William Cowper display at the town's museum (see page 105).

George Borrow (1803-81) was an eccentric character, more at home with the gypsies, whose language he learned, than in polite society. He was born at Dumpling Green, East Dereham, and briefly attended Norwich Grammar School. He was no academic but he was a clever linguist, and at eighteen he understood ten languages. For many years he worked for the British and Foreign Bible Society, which took him to many countries including Spain and Russia. His best-known books are *Lavengro* and *The Bible in Spain*. It was he who coined the phrase 'A fine old city' when referring to Norwich. He married a comfortably-off widow and settled in Oulton Broad, where he remained after she died. He died in poverty in his cottage at Oulton Broad but was buried with his wife in London. The Bishop Bonner Cottages Museum (see page 105) has a display of Borrow memorabilia.

Anna Sewell (1820-78) was a more homely author. She was born in Great Yarmouth to a strict Quaker family and became lame as a result of a childhood fall. The family was not wealthy but she was taken to Germany for a cure which enabled her to walk again. Inspired by Horace Bushell's *Essay on Animals,* she wrote *Black Beauty* in an attempt to improve the treatment of horses. It was an immediate success and became a children's classic. Her birthplace may be seen on Priory Green in Yarmouth (see page 25).

Captain Frederick Marryat (1792-1848),

The home of Anna Sewell in Great Yarmouth.

the author of another children's classic, *The Children of the New Forest* (1847), retired to Norfolk at the end of a successful naval career. He bought the Manor House and 700 acres (283 hectares) of land at Langham in 1841. He was already an established author of adult fiction before turning to writing for children. A year after *The Children of the New Forest* was published he died and is buried at Langham.

Another popular author was **Rider Haggard** (1856-1925), who was born at Bradenham Hall, the eighth child of a moderately wealthy Norfolk squire. As a young man he found it difficult to settle to a profession and served in the army in South Africa during the Zulu and Boer Wars. On returning to England

with his wife and son, he studied law. He began writing for financial reasons, drawing on his experiences in Africa. His first book, *Dawn*, written in five months, was well reviewed and sold well. His next two books, *King Solomon's Mines* (1885) and *She* (1886), were instant bestsellers. He returned to Norfolk to live at Ditchingham Hall near the Suffolk border and pursued his interests as a rural reformer, advocating afforestation long before environmental concerns were popular. He died at Ditchingham and there is a memorial window to him in St Mary's church.

Letters and diaries

The *Paston Letters* (1422-1509) provide a vivid account of the life on a small estate at Paston in north Norfolk of a family involved in affairs of state at a time of change as the middle ages came to a close. At Paston the beautiful thatched barn built by Sir William Paston in 1582 survives and later Pastons are commemorated in St Margaret's church. The Strangers' Club in Elm Hill, Norwich, occupies the site of the town house of Margaret Paston.

Two centuries later, at Weston Longville, the worldly **Parson James Woodforde** (1740-1803) recorded his day-to-day life in his thatched parsonage, since demolished, which was alive with rats but nevertheless the scene of much conviviality. His delightful diaries give a lively account of all aspects of rural life from dinners with the lesser gentry to the feasts he provided for the local farmers after the tithes had been paid.

A great musician

John Wilbye (1574-1638), said to be the greatest English madrigalist, was born at Diss to a prosperous family of tanners. His musical skills were recognised by the Kitson family of nearby Hengrave Hall, just over the border in Suffolk. The Kitsons were a remarkably musical family and Wilbye entered their service. He travelled with them to London and so became acquainted with other musicians of the day. Wilbye prospered as a musician, publishing books of his compositions, and also as a businessman. He is not known to have composed any music after

1609, for reasons which are not understood.

Landscape gardener

The building of the many grand houses in Norfolk, their furnishing and the landscaping of their parks attracted many great architects, designers and landscape gardeners. One of them, perhaps the greatest landscape gardener of the eighteenth century, was a Norfolk man, **Humphry Repton** (1752-1818). He spent the early part of his life in Norwich and then at Sustead Hall and did not take up landscape gardening until the age of 39. He quickly built up a reputation for meticulous planning and artistic excellence. He worked on at least sixteen estates in Norfolk, nowhere more successfully than at Sheringham Park (see page 103).

The Norwich School of Artists

In the early nineteenth century Norwich was the centre of a group of artists linked by their common aim of basing their work on direct observation and departing from the prettiness and sentiment of the art of the previous century. They were also linked by family ties or as masters and pupils. There is a magnificent collection of their work at the Norwich Castle Museum.

John Crome (1768-1821) was an early member of the group. He was the son of a weaver and was apprenticed as a sign painter. As a young man he was influenced by Dutch paintings he had seen at the home of a Norwich master weaver. His paintings achieved a freshness of vision without losing their technical excellence. Among his pupils, in addition to his own four children, were James Stark and George Vincent. His contemporaries included the Hodgsons, the Ladbrokes, the Ninhams and the highly talented Stannard family, among whom were two women artists. Many of the artists came from craft backgrounds: the Starks, for example, were textile dyers, the Vincents shawl manufacturers and another important watercolourist, John Thirtle (1777-1839), was a carver and gilder.

John Sell Cotman (1777-1839) is the most famous of the Norwich School artists. His watercolours have been described as the most perfect examples ever made in Europe. He was the son of a haberdasher. He left Norwich to work as an artist for various patrons in London, travelling with them to Wales and Yorkshire, and as a result his paintings are not restricted to Norfolk subjects. He was, however, based in Norwich for much of his life and exhibited with the Norwich Society of Artists. In 1811 he became its president. For twelve years from 1812 he was employed by a Yarmouth banker as an art master and during this time he travelled to Normandy to sketch architecture for his patron. Cotman's misfortune, he said, was to 'skulk through life as a drawing master and pattern drawer to young ladies' but he nevertheless produced a remarkable body of work which is more and more admired as the years go by.

Saints and martyrs

The details of the lives of many early Norfolk saints, such as St Walstan of Bawburgh, St Withburga of Dereham, St Edmund, who led

Edith Cavell's grave at Norwich Cathedral.

TO THE PURE
AND HOLY MEMORY
OF

EDITH CAVELL
WHO GAVE HER LIFE FOR ENGLAND
12ᵀᴴ OCTOBER 1915

HER NAME LIVETH FOR EVERMORE

troops against the Danish invaders at Thetford, or the apocryphal St William of Norwich, are lost in the mists of time. The Catholic martyr **St Robert Southwell** (1562-95), the Jesuit poet, who was born at Horsham, and **St Henry Walpole** (1558-95), who was born at Docking, are real enough. Both died for their Catholic faith in Elizabethan times.

Edith Cavell (1865-1915) was shot by a German firing squad in Brussels during the First World War after helping hundreds of British soldiers escape from occupied Belgium. Her famous last words, recorded on her statue in Norwich, were 'Patriotism is not enough'. She was born at Swardeston in Norfolk and became a governess and then a nurse. Chance took her to Brussels, where she became matron of a teaching hospital and virtually established the Belgian nursing service. When war was declared and Belgium occupied by the Germans, she became leader of an escape organisation. She was later arrested, found guilty of spying and executed.

Natural history

E. A. Ellis (1909-86) was born in Guernsey of Norfolk parents but returned to Norfolk to become Keeper of Natural History at Norwich Castle Museum from 1928 to 1956. He lived with his family at Wheatfen Broad, Surlingham, in a remote cottage among the reeds. His weekly notes in the *Eastern Daily Press* and his many other writings, as well as his radio and television broadcasts, vividly describe the world of nature, particularly the fens and waterways of Norfolk. He was awarded an honorary doctorate by the University of East Anglia. Since his death, Wheatfen has been turned into a permanent nature reserve with the help of the 'Ted Ellis Trust'.

Margaret Fountaine (1862-1940) was a less conventional naturalist as her book *Love Among the Butterflies* demonstrates. She was born at Southacre, the daughter of a clergyman, but as a young woman she ran off with an Irish singer. She pursued him abroad and when he rejected her she began her life of travel, romantic affairs and a quest for butterflies. She eventually met a Syrian dragoman, with whom she travelled for the next 28 years. Her book was found with her collection of butterflies stored away in Norwich Castle Museum (see page 109) and became a bestseller when published in 1980.

The Dukes of Norfolk

For the past two hundred years the Dukes of Norfolk and other members of the Howard family have been associated with Arundel Castle in West Sussex and Carlton Towers in North Yorkshire rather than with the county from which they derive their ducal title. The family first came into prominence in the thirteenth century when Sir William Howard of East Winch near King's Lynn (where family tombs may still be seen) became a Chief Justice under Edward I. Over the next two hundred years the family acquired much land in East Anglia, said to be the largest private estate in England. Sir John Howard was created the first Duke of Norfolk by Richard III and at various times Howards have had other titles bestowed on them. One of them, the Earl of Surrey, had a large house near present-day Surrey Street in Norwich. The third Duke of Norfolk built a mansion at Kenninghall on the Norfolk/Suffolk border; part of a wing survives as a farmhouse. The fences at Kenninghall were thrown down during Kett's rebellion in 1549 and the Earl of Surrey's house in Norwich was sacked. Later, in the Civil War, the house was destroyed. The third Duke also built a palace on the site of the Grey Friars' monastery in Norwich and he encouraged Flemish weavers to settle in the city. During the Reformation the Dukes' estates were confiscated because of their refusal to abandon Catholicism, and they also suffered for their support for the Stuarts during the Civil War. After the restoration of Charles II their fortunes improved. Their Norwich palace was rebuilt as a town house and Charles II was entertained there. The site of the palace in Duke Street is now a car park. In 1711, after further trouble with the city authorities, the eighth Duke demolished much of his palace and left Norwich. The fifteenth Duke, however, made a spectacular gesture to Norwich when he built the Roman Catholic cathedral (1884-1910), one of the most ambitious churches ever to be built in England by a private individual.

Royalty

Norfolk has had many close connections with the Royal Family over the centuries. Queen Isabella was banished to Castle Rising. Henry VII stayed at Oxburgh Hall and embroideries by Mary, Queen of Scots, are displayed there. Queen Elizabeth I spent part of her childhood at Shelton and Anne Boleyn, second queen of Henry VIII, lived at Blickling as a girl. No monarch had stronger ties with Norfolk than Edward VII. He bought the Sandringham Estate (see page 102) in 1860 and while Sandringham House was being rebuilt for him in 1870 he used his great friend Lord Suffield's Gunton Hall in north Norfolk as a shooting lodge. Subsequently, most of Europe's royalty have been entertained at Sandringham House and it has remained a favourite royal residence to this day.

The town sign in East Dereham depicts St Withburga protecting deer from the hunt.

14
Further reading

Anderson, Verity. *The Northrepps Grandchildren.* Hodder & Stoughton, 1968.

Ayer, A. J. *Thomas Paine.* Secker & Warburg, 1958.

Bennett, Joan. *Sir Thomas Browne.* Cambridge University Press, 1962.

Clarke, W. G. *The Breckland Wilds.* Heffer, 1937.

Day, J. Wentworth. *Portrait of the Broads.* Hale, 1967.

Dutt, W. A. *King's Lynn with Its Surroundings.* 1905.

Dymond, David. *The Norfolk Landscape.* Hodder & Stoughton, 1958.

Ellis, E. A. *The Broads.* Collins, 1952.

Evans, George Ewart. *The Crooked Scythe.* Faber & Faber, 1993. (An anthology of oral history.)

Fenn, Ida. *Tales of a Countryman.* Reeve, 1973. (In dialect.)

Fowler, Eric. *The Best of Johnathon Mardle.* Albion, 1982.

Hales, Jane. *The East Wind.* East Anglia Publications, 1969.

Hopkinson, B. *Norfolk in Colour.* Barbara Hopkinson Books, 1989.

Jebb, Miles. *East Anglia. A National Trust Anthology.* National Trust, 1980.

Kennett, D. H. *Norfolk Village.* Hale, 1983.

Ketton-Cremer, R. W. *Felbrigg. The Story of a House.* Hart-Davis, 1962.

Malster, Robert. *The Broads.* Phillimore, 1993.

Mortlock, D. P., and Roberts, C. V. *Norfolk Churches* (two volumes). 1985.

Mottram, R. H. *If Stones Could Speak.* EP Publishing, 1985.

Patterson, A. *Seaside Scribblings.* Jarrold, 1890.

Pevsner, N. *The Buildings of England: North West and South Norfolk* and *North East Norfolk and Norwich* (two volumes). Penguin, 1962.

Richards, Paul. *King's Lynn.* Phillimore, 1990.

Rider-Haggard, Lilias. *A Norfolk Notebook.* Sutton, 1946.

Tilbrook, R., and Timpson, J. *Norwich: A Fine City.* Jarrold, 1988.

Timpson, J. *Timpson's Travels in East Anglia.* Heinemann, 1990.

Wade-Martins, Peter. *An Historical Atlas of Norfolk.* Norfolk Museum Services, 1992.

Wade-Martins, Susanna. *A History of Norfolk.* Chichester, 1984.

Wade-Martins, Susanna. *A Changing Countryside 1780-1914.* Phillimore, 1988.

Williamson, Henry. *The Story of a Norfolk Farm.* Clive, reprinted 1986 (first published 1941).

Winkley, George. *The Country Houses of Norfolk.* Tyndale & Panda, 1986.

Women's Institutes. *The Norfolk Village Book.* Countryside Books, 1990.

Woodforde, James. *Diary of a Country Parson 1758-1781.* Oxford University Press, reprinted 1978.

Yaxley, David. *Portrait of Norfolk.* Hale, 1977.

15
Tourist information centres

An asterisk * denotes offices open only in summer.

Broads Authority: 18 Colegate, Norwich NR3 1BQ. Telephone: 0603 610734.
Cromer: Old Town Hall, Prince of Wales Road, Cromer NR27 9HS. Telephone: 0263 512497.
Diss*: Meres Mouth, Mere Street, Diss IP22 3AG. Telephone: 0379 650523.
Fakenham: Red Lion House, Market Place, Fakenham NR21 8DJ. Telephone: 0328 51981.
Great Yarmouth: Department of Publicity and Entertainments, 1 South Quay, Great Yarmouth NR30 2PX. Telephone: 0493 946345.
Hoveton*: Station Road, Hoveton, Wroxham NR12 5AH. Telephone: 0603 782281.
Hunstanton: The Green, Hunstanton PE36 5AH. Telephone: 0485 532610.
King's Lynn: The Old Gaol House, Saturday Market, King's Lynn PE30 5AS. Telephone: 0553 763044.
Mundesley*: Shoppers' Car Park, Mundesley NR11 8JH. Telephone: 0263 721070.
Norwich: The Guildhall, Gaol Hill, Norwich NR2 1NF. Telephone: 0603 666071.
Ranworth*: The Staithe, Market Square, Ranworth NR13 6HY. Telephone: 060549 453.
Santon Downham: Forestry Commission Office, Santon Downham, Suffolk IP27 0JJ. Telephone: 0482 810271.
Sheringham: Station Car Park, Sheringham NR26 8RA. Telephone: 0263 824329.
Swaffham*: Ceres Bookshop, 16-20 London Street, Swaffham PE37 7DG. Telephone: 0760 22255.
Thetford: Ancient House Museum, White Hart Street, Thetford IP24 1AA. Telephone: 0842 752599.
Walsingham: Shirehall Museum, Common Place, Walsingham NR22 6DB. Telephone: 0328 820510.
Wells-next-the-Sea: Wells Centre, Staithe Road, Wells-next-the-Sea NR23 1AN. Telephone: 0328 710885.

Index
Page numbers in italics refer to illustrations.